Complete
Wheel and Tire
Buyer's Guide

Brad Bowling

Published by

 **krause publications**
An F&W Publications Company

700 East State Street • Iola, WI 54990-0001
715-445-2214 • 888-457-2873
www.krause.com

Please, call or write us for our free catalog of publications.
Our toll-free number to place an order or obtain a free catalog is 800-258-0929
or please us our regular business telephone 715-445-2214.

ISBN: 0-87349-661-2
Library of Congress Number: 2003108887
Printed in the United States of America

Edited by Karen O'Brien
Designed by Matthew DeRhodes and Brian Brogaard

On the Cover
Front cover: Two JDM (Japanese Domestic Market) beauties sit low on their Volk Racing
wheels and low-profile rubber. (Photo Volk Racing)
Back cover: A gigantic Ford Excursion sits high above a set of chromed 20-inch KMC
wheels and 305/40R20 Nitto NT404 tires. (Photo Brad Bowling)

CONTENTS

This Celica has The Sit. (Photo ALT)

The Sit and How to Get it

Either your car has The Sit or it doesn't.

You know what The Sit is. The Sit makes your ride look like a street fighter ready to get busy—it makes it bristle with attitude and calls attention to itself without having to say a word. When your car has The Sit it no longer resembles a machine driving down the street—it prowls like a wild animal with a purpose.

No matter what other modifications you make to a car, if the hot motor, neon tubes, whack paint job, and custom interior aren't backed up by the right set of rims and rubber...well, you ain't got Sit.

You know what The Sit is. You just may not know how to get it yet.

Between the covers of this book is an education on wheels and tires, the two most important elements of a good Sit.

Cars today are better than they ever have been. Performance, handling, and comfort have never been more successfully combined in automotive history, but built-in

compromises keep us enthusiasts from buying the cars and trucks we really want to own. Even the sportiest coupes, sedans, and musclecars still come from the factory with wheels that are too narrow, tires whose sidewalls are too tall, and enough air in the fenders to supply an underwater city. The luxury SUVs we crave look like expensive roller skates riding on their "little" 17s.

The new crop of bodies may look great and have the creature comforts we need, but they Sit high like a nervous schoolmarm who just heard a mouse squeak. This explains why the aftermarket parts industry is a mega-million dollar treasure chest.

Wheels are the most obvious visual cues on a car when seen from a 3/4 angle or profile. Their size, design, offset, and finish speak volumes about the style of the vehicle's owner. They also reveal whether the car is built for speed (wearing super lightweight silver BBS three-piece alloys, for example) or to be a boulevard cruiser (24-inch chrome Davin spinners). As discussed elsewhere, the most important dimensions to consider when buying wheels for

So does this Volkswagen Beetle. (Photo Borbet)

the perfect Sit are diameter, width, and offset. In the course of researching this book, we cataloged 150 individual brands of wheels sold in the United States, enough to give you a good start toward a purchasing decision.

Any upgrade in wheel size—whether in diameter or width—brings with it the need for different tires. People traditionally have their loyalties and preferences when it comes to manufacturers, but today it is nearly impossible to buy a truly unacceptable tire as long as it has a well-known brand name. Because there are so many different types of cars, trucks and drivers out there, tires cover a vast range of needs, from ultra high-performance Ferraris to "are we there yet?" Honda minivans. The hottest ticket right now is the large-diameter, low-profile performance tire, especially among the truck and SUV crowd. How do you know if this trendy rubber is right for your application? This book will fill you in on the different types of tires and their characteristics. Highlighted in that chapter are two dozen

tire lines sold in the U.S.

The Sit usually requires lowering the chassis with springs and custom-made suspension components which, along with brake systems on modern cars, are no longer a one-size-fits-all proposition. Fitment problems can arise if the proper equipment is not used. Because technical information about suspension modifications can fill several books of this size, we will not be discussing the subject except to recommend lowering if changing wheels and tires do not by themselves deliver the look or ride you are seeking.

Achieving The Sit can cost anywhere from $300 to $15,000, so consider this book to be cheap insurance against a bad investment. The more you know about the product, the less it costs.

Brad Bowling
Charlotte, N.C.

ACKNOWLEDGMENTS

It's amazing what they can do with a circle.
- Heath Culp

A project of this type could never come together without the input, advice and help of many people. Unlike a book of fiction, where the information flows out of the writer's head and onto the paper, researching 100 years of wheel and tire production in the United States requires many visits to the library, and countless hours scanning the Internet but—most important of all—contact with real human beings.

The first step on my 10,000-mile journey began with a drive to South Bend, Ind., where I spent the day with John Rastetter of The Tire Rack. Rastetter is the director of tire information services for a company that, frankly, is run by a bunch of car nuts thinly disguised as a hugely successful corporation. I enjoyed meeting several members of The Tire Rack's very knowledgeable online and phone sales team, some of whom I photographed with their cars for this book. Speaking of photography, Elizabeth Pavelski shared with me nearly 100 of her beautiful wheel and tire studio images and Matt Edmonds, director of marketing, coordinated the assembly of that package. The Tire Rack can be contacted at 888-541-1777 or through

The Tire Rack not only sells wheels and tires—they test them as well.

www.tirerack.com.

I've known Punchy Whitaker since buying a set of wheels from him after moving to Charlotte in 1995. The wheels were used Mazda alloy rims for an '86 RX-7 I was restoring. Over the phone Punchy told me he was asking $100 for the set, which sounded like a good deal. When I went to pick them up, he pulled the perfectly good set out of storage and said, "I'll let you have 'em for $80." I've been a customer ever since. Whitaker Wheel & Tire's current collection of buildings stuffed with everything from standard passenger rubber and steel factory rims to the latest 24-inch chrome wheels and 35-profile tires have been a magnet for Carolinas car enthusiasts since the 1960s. The aftermarket wheel industry is a healthy giant, and Punchy monitors its pulse with amazing accuracy. He is an old school horse trader businessman who buys low and sells low, but with a profit for his troubles. Volume is the name of his game. I interviewed Punchy to get his input and observations for this book, and he let me set up a small studio in his showroom where I spent the day photographing hundreds of wheels and answering questions from customers who thought I worked there.

Punchy is a hands-on wheel and tire dealer. Somehow he always knows where every item in his inventory is located.

Morrison Motor Co. is a never-ending source of great photo subjects. Gary Morrison owns three 1959 Cadillacs with modern chrome wheels.

Help for the day came from photo assistant Crystal Carraway and Punchy's knowledgeable sales staff, especially Heath Culp. Punchy can always be found at 590 Concord Pkwy. N., Concord, N.C. 28027 or by phone at 704-876-6174.

It seems I can't write a book without making several stops at Morrison Motor Co. in Concord. Jimmy Morrison and his family have run this very successful collector car dealership since the 1960s, originally specializing in Corvettes. Since his lot is usually overflowing with the aforementioned Chevrolet sports cars, Mustangs, Camaros, SUVs and Harley-Davidson motorcycles, there were plenty of sharp vehicles wearing aftermarket wheels when I visited with my camera equipment. Jimmy, Jay, Mike, Greg, Gary, Larry, Ashlyn, and Barbara are some of the nicest people I've met in the car business, and the Morrisons were once again generous in loaning me vehicles for photo shoots. Morrison Motor Co. is located at 1170 Old Charlotte Rd., Concord, NC 28027 and can be contacted at 704-782-7716 or through their Web site at www.morrisonmotorco.com.

During research and photography for my book I dropped by Muffler Masters, the shop that has put about a half-dozen dual exhaust systems on my cars and trucks. I had some

questions about repairing tires, so Bobby Franklin let me follow Billy Owens through fixing a flat and balancing the wheel and tire afterwards. These are also the guys I get to do alignments, brake work and the occasional trailer hitch installation, so I have great trust in their information and advice that appears here. They can be found at 2205 S. Cannon Blvd., Kannapolis, NC 28083 or by phoning 704-938-1146. Look for the gigantic muffler in the air—you can't miss it.

Jim Mayfield, the director of General brand management at Continental Tire in Charlotte, entertained my questions for more than an hour recently. Getting the inside story directly from a tire manufacturer was a tremendous help in writing that chapter and I appreciate

Good office help is hard to find.

Thanks to the guys at Muffler Masters for letting me hound them with my camera and tape recorder.

the time he volunteered for the book.

Brian Babcock, president of Automotive Anything, has a great custom parts shop and was very helpful in lining up customer cars for me to photograph. His place is at 12052 University City Blvd., Hwy. 49 @ County Line Plaza, Harrisburg, NC 28075. Automotive Anything's phone number is 704-455-1119 or visit the Web site at www.automotiveanything.com.

Roger Jackman at H&R Springs provided assistance in the section on spacers that appears in the wheel chapter. H&R can be reached at 888-827-8881 or through its Web site at www.hrsprings.com.

Michael Burns spent a day and half on the phone with sales and p.r. representatives of wheel and tire companies reminding everyone to send product photography.

Finally, I want to say thanks to my wife Heather for pulling me away from the computer when she could tell I really needed to take a break and to my furry assistant Lizzie—even though she has no office skills whatsoever and the only words we have in common are "treat" and "go outside."

Brian Martin is a frequent customer of Automotive Anything, and his modified Dodge Dakota attests to that fact.

SECTION ONE
TIRES

GOODYEAR AND DUNLOP—THE MEN BEHIND THE TIRES

The story of the wheel is the history of modern civilization. 3500 B.C.E. is the approximate date early man discovered the beautifully simple potential of the circle. Since that time, wheels have been made of stone, wood, steel, aluminum, carbon fiber, and many other materials.

It wasn't, however, until the 19th century A.D. that a suitable soft "wrap" could be invented for those hard wheels. Two men did more to put the world on rubber tires than anyone else—Charles Goodyear, an obsessed inventor; and John Boyd Dunlop, a part-time tinkerer.

GOODYEAR

The Charles Goodyear story is similar to that of Thomas Edison's or the Wright Brothers'. Like the inventor of the light bulb and hundreds of everyday products, Goodyear was tenacious about pursuing his ideas to the point of bankrupting himself and his family and ruining his health. Goodyear was the vanguard of a movement whose followers were convinced that miraculous properties of natural rubber had not yet been fully realized in the early 1800s—just as Orville and Wilbur's meticulous research would later give birth to the world-changing science of aviation.

Unlike the Edison and Wright stories, Goodyear would be in and out of debtors' prison all his life and eventually die owing creditors $200,000. To understand how the invention of one man led to the staggering fortunes of those who followed, it is necessary to understand that for a

At the turn of the 19th century, it was as much fun to make tires as it was to change them. (Photo Goodyear)

period in the 1830s rubber companies had as much investor interest and financial potential as the Internet craze of the 1990s. The new waterproof gum from Brazil had captured America's interest briefly as a possible new material for mass-producing weatherproof clothing, baskets, nautical equipment, and other handy items.

In other words, they envisioned the world we have today, but there were a few hurdles to clear first. Unprocessed rubber had one major drawback as consumer commodities go; it could freeze solid in the winter and turn to runny goo in the heat of summer. Not exactly the kind of material you want your raincoat made from.

Goodyear was attempting to sell the manager of a Roxbury India Rubber Co. retail store in New York on a valve he had envented for rubber life preserves when he discovered the company's entire stock had become a stinking pile of gum due to the heat. By this time, many other startup rubber companies had experienced the same self-destructing tendency of their inventories and all went out of business.

Somehow, Goodyear got it in his head that the road to his and America's future was paved with rubber but—like alchemists attempting to turn base metals into gold—no one had figured out the transformation method. During one of his many jail sentences for debt, Goodyear had his wife deliver some raw rubber and a rolling pin so he could pass the time kneading and studying his miracle gum. Once out of jail, he experimented with adding a talc-like magnesia powder to the raw rubber to remove its tackiness and was pleased with the results. With a friend bankrolling his venture, Goodyear produced a few hundred pairs of rubber overshoes in his family's kitchen, only to watch them melt in the summer. The stubborn inventor was forced to move from his Philadelphia home due to the odors created by his experiments. He set up shop in an apartment bedroom in New York to continue.

The next stage of his success was the idea of mixing magnesia and quicklime with rubber and boiling the mixture, but still no "Eureka!" moment. He spent his time between experiments decorating and painting his rubber products and contemplating where the work might be taking him.

One fateful day he ran out of raw rubber and used nitric acid to remove the bronze paint from one of his crafts so as to use it in an experiment. The object turned black on contact with the acid, and Goodyear threw it away. Retrieving it from the trash a few days later, he noticed the rubber felt smooth and dry—exactly the effect he had been looking for.

His new nitric-acid process looked to be money in the bank. When Goodyear won a government contract for 150 rubber mailbags, he manufactured and stored them, then celebrated by taking his long-suffering family on a month-long vacation. On his return he discovered the summer heat had... well, you can guess by now. The surface, having been treated with nitric acid, was smooth and perfect, but the underside was again a runny mess.

In February of 1839, without a penny to his name, "Eureka!" finally came to Charles Goodyear. He was showing some skeptical general store patrons the product of his latest experiment—at this point sulphur had been thrown in to the mix—when some of the sticky gum fell onto the hot stove and began to burn. When Goodyear scraped it off, he noticed it had cured like leather instead of running like molasses, creating the world's first weatherproof rubber and modern plastic.

The rest of Goodyear's life was spent further developing his rubber recipe and finding myriad new uses for the compound. Unfortunately for his family's financial situation, his focus on the invention prevented him from making sound business decisions (such as applying for patents in a timely manner) and he died with only his name

to his credit in 1860.

He and his family were in no way involved with the company that would be founded four decades later bearing the Goodyear name. That company would become one of the world's largest corporations and eventually rake in billions of dollars annually through sales of tires, rubber sheeting, hoses, and a multitude of diverse manufacturing interests.

DUNLOP

John Boyd Dunlop was a successful veterinarian with a practice in Belfast, Ireland, when he stepped onto the rubber road of fortune that had eluded Charles Goodyear. One day in 1888 Dunlop was watching his son struggle with his bicycle because its solid rubber tires—while better than the previous century's metal or wood rims—did not allow him to navigate over the cobbled texture of what passed for a sidewalk.

The vet realized that compressed air would make the rubber tire more pliable over odd-shaped surfaces and more comfortable for his son. He covered a rubber inner tube with a jacket of linen tape and sealed it all with an outer rubber tread. The tire was then attached to the wheel by rubber cementing flaps on the jacket and pressurized by a soccer ball pump.

Dunlop wasn't the first person to put together such a device—in fact, he wasn't even the first Scotsman to do so. Robert William Thomson had patented a tubeless tire design in 1846, but Dunlop improved on the idea and made it practical for production.

Realizing he was sitting on a gold mine, Dunlop quickly went into business producing tires. In 1896, he sold his patent and interest in the company for 3 million pounds. Within 10 years of its patent, the pneumatic tire replaced solid rubber tires in almost all applications. The Dunlop company was eventually acquired, ironically enough, by Goodyear Tire and Rubber.

Goodyear and Dunlop, the men, did more to put the world on soft rubber tires than anyone else in history. Although there have been great strides in tire technology since, it was these two pioneers—very much unalike in method and personality—whose lives and work most impacted the way we live today.

TIRE HISTORY HIGHLIGHTS

1839 — Charles Goodyear discovers vulcanization, the process that makes rubber durable enough to be used commercially.

1872 — Giovanni Battista Pirelli establishes Pirelli & C. in Milan, Italy, and soon thereafter is producing rubber goods.

1888 — John Boyd Dunlop of Belfast, Ireland, invents the pneumatic tire.

1889 — Brothers Edouard and André Michelin create a rubber company and name it after themselves in Clermont-Ferrand, France.

1891 — Michelin patents the removable tire, one of the truly innovative leaps forward for the industry. The process was developed after Edouard Michelin spent 3

"Bibendum" is the original name of the Michelin Man.

hours repairing a bicycle tire for a visiting cyclist.

1892 — U.S. Rubber Co. is founded, eventually becomes Uniroyal.

1894 — Edwin S. Kelly founds The Rubber Tire Wheel Company in Springfield, Ohio, to produce carriage tires.

1894 — The first rubber tires appear for horse drawn carriages and begin to replace the age-old iron-bound wheels.

1895 — The Michelin brothers build a car specifically to introduce their pneumatic tires. Known as "The Eclair" (French for "lightning"), the car competes in the Paris-Bordeaux-Paris race.

1898 — Bibendum (aka Michelin Man) is born. The character eventually becomes recognized the world over, in the same league with Ronald McDonald and Mickey Mouse.

1899 — Goodyear adds automobile tires to its original product line of bicycle and carriage tires and horseshoe pads.

1900 — Michelin produces its first edition of the *Red Guide*—a run of 35,000.

1900 — Goodyear exhibits its first solid tires at the Auto Show in New York.

1900 — The Firestone Tire & Rubber Co. is founded in Akron, Ohio, by Harvey S. Firestone.

1901 — Goodyear's Wingfoot logo appears for the first time. It represents the mythological figure known to the Romans as Mercury and to the Greeks as Hermes, whose chief responsibilities were trade, commerce, and delivery.

1901 — Goodyears debut in competition, driven by Henry Ford.

1903 — Goodyear patents first tubeless tire.

1903 — Michelin creates its first tire for motorcycles.

1904 — Goodyear patents the removable wheel, which quickly replaces the one-piece "clincher" design.

1906 — Goodyear produces the first quickly detachable straight-side tire.

1907 — Goodyear begins selling a cord tire for electric automobiles.

1908 — The dual wheel is invented and increases the load capacity of trucks and heavier vehicles.

1908 — Goodyear introduces its first All-Weather Tread tire, with diamond-shaped blocks for increased wet-weather traction.

1910 — Michelin prints the first in its now-famous series of road maps.

1911 — Ray Harroun wins the inaugural Indy 500. His Marmon Wasp is shod with Firestone tires.

1912 — Goodyear blimp debuts.

1913 — The invention of the removable steel wheel single handedly gives birth to the concept of a convenient spare tire.

1914 — The Rubber Tire Wheel Co. becomes The Kelly-Springfield Tire Co and specializes in pneumatic tires for automobiles.

1915 — Carbon black, a World War I substitute for zinc oxide, is introduced to tire compounds.

1917 — Michelin creates its first tire tread made with black rubber. The addition of carbon powder proves to be a leap forward in roadholding and resistance to wear.

1919 — Cords replace crisscrossing sheets of rubberized canvas to create a tire carcass with greater strength and life.

1921 — Goodyear introduces its rut-proof tire, creating the off-the-road market.

1927 — Goodyear introduces its first all-weather tire with a ribbed tread design for greater stability and applies for synthetic rubber patents.

1923 — Michelin's Comfort is the first low-pressure touring tire, with a useful life of 9,500 miles.

1930 — Michelin patents the built-in tube tire, which eventually evolved into a tubeless design.

1930 — Goodyear begins selling its low-pressure Airwheel tire to Ford and

Chevrolet. It was originally designed for aviation.

1931 — The Bridgestone Tire Co. Ltd. was founded in Kurume, Japan, by Shojiro Ishibashi. Ishibashi's surname means "stone bridge" in English.

1932 — In an era when tires were notoriously short-lived, Michelin's introduction of the 19,000-mile Super Comfort very low-pressure tire was big news.

1934 — The Super Comfort Stop, introduced by Michelin, features holding strips on the tread that reduce skidding under wet conditions.

1934 — Goodyear introduces the first studded mud and snow tires.

1935 — Goodyear acquires Kelly-Springfield.

1937 — Goodyear tests and produces the first synthetic rubber tire for the military.

1938 — Michelin's Metalic tire marks the first useful combination of steel wire and rubber. It found immediate favor with manufacturers of heavy-duty vehicles, and was a major step toward the eventual development of the radial tire.

1938 — Goodyear introduces first rayon passenger tires.

1941-46 — Tire and automobile manufacturing facilities in the United States were turned over to the government's control for the duration of World War II.

1946 — Michelin patents a design for the radial tire, which would go on sale as the "X" in 1949.

1947 — Goodyear produces first nylon belts for tires and Super-Cushion tire which required only 24 psi of air pressure.

1948 — Pirelli introduces its Cinturato radial tire.

1952 — Goodyear's Suburbanite winter tire is introduced.

1954 — Goodyear introduces complete line of tubeless tires.

1956 — Goodyear announces an early version of its current run-flat system called the Captive-Air Safety Tire. It is advertised as "the tire with the built-in spare." The company also introduces a line of tires for a little regional phenomenon known as NASCAR stock car racing.

1964 — Uniroyal introduces its Tiger mascot.

1965 — Michelin creates the XAS, the first tire with asymmetric structure and tread, for racing.

1965 — Goodyear introduces radial-ply tires in a full range of sizes to the auto manufacturers. Winter tires with Safety Spikes also debuted from the company.

1967 — Goodyear debuts its Custom Wide Tread Polyglas tire, which will become standard equipment on many new 1969 cars.

1967 — Bridgestone enters the U.S. market.

1969 — Yokohama enters the U.S. market.

1970 — Goodyear tires drive on the moon. Apollo 14's Modularized Equipment Transporter (MET) is shod with Goodyear XLT tires.

1971 — Pirelli and Dunlop begin a decade of cooperative development ventures.

1974 — Goodyear introduces a winter tire designed for use without metal studs, the F32 All Winter Radial.

1977 — Goodyear introduces the first all-season radial, the Tiempo, and an elliptic tire design with fuel-saving potential.

1978 — Goodyear pioneers rubber recycling in new ways by creating more than 2,000 artificial reefs from old tires to protect marine life.

1980 — Goodyear announces the Arriva all-season radial.

1981 — Goodyear debuts its Eagle family of high-performance tires at Daytona.

1982 — All new car models sold in the U.S. are equipped with radial tires.

1984 — Goodyear introduces its third-generation all-season radial, Vector.

1987 — Goodyear's ZR-S is the industry's first Z-rated high-performance tire, which means it is designed to operate at speeds greater than 149 miles per hour. The company also becomes

the first American producer of 17-inch tires for OEM applications by putting its Eagle ZR40 Gatorback on the 1988 Chevrolet Corvette.

1988 — Bridgestone acquires Firestone.

1989 — Goodyear develops SIBR, a synthetic rubber that raises its Eagle tires' heat resistance.

1992 — Michelin produces the first "green" tire, a design that greatly reduces rolling resistance and nets higher gas mileage.

1992 — Goodyear introduces the Aquatred design with advanced water-dispersing tread. Emergency Mobility Technology (EMT)—also known generically as run-flat—is introduced. Its first application is for the Chevrolet Corvette.

1998 — Michelin begins work on its PAX run-flat system.

1998 — Goodyear introduces a new passenger car steel belt technology known as Ultra-Tensile Steel Wire. It's first appearance is in the Eagle Aquasteel EMT and Eagle F1 Steel tires.

2000 — Goodyear and Michelin agree to combine their PAX and EMT system development.

2000 — Goodyear introduces the Aquatred 3, the next evolution of the company's successful water channel technology.

2000 — Goodyear introduces the Kelly Navigator Platinum TE, a touring tire that features an 80,000-mile treadwear warranty.

(Photo Goodyear)

HOW MODERN RADIAL TIRES ARE MADE

Creating a radial tire is like cooking an incredibly complex casserole. There is a grocery list of very specific ingredients to be mixed, stirred and processed, then the whole concoction is heated in a shape-giving container until the various components have blended into one finished product.

A worker inspects a "green" tire before it is vulcanized and given its final shape in the mold. (Photo Goodyear)

Ingredients for a radial tire include more than 30 different types of rubber, cord and wire, and big helpings of pigments and chemicals. Developing just the right compound starts with basic rubbers and process oils, carbon black, pigments, antioxidants, accelerators, and other additives chosen for their various properties.

Different manufacturers have different "recipes" and systems for creating a tire—neither of which they are willing to divulge. What follows is a generalized step-by-step of the tire-building process.

Banbury machines—think giant kitchen blenders that can mix under tremendous heat and pressure—suck in this soup and spit out a hot, black gummy compound that is shaped into long, flat bands of rubber. From the banbury, these bands will be processed into six main components that will eventually make up the bulk of a tire's casing.

1. A tuber shapes the flat strips into tread rubber, which is measured, cooled, and cut to precise lengths.

2. Another tuber converts the strips into sidewalls, which can be combined at this stage with white rubber for a whitewall or white lettering.

3. A calendar mill creates the plies by combining thin sheets of rubber with rayon, nylon or polyester fibers.

4. Belts are created when steel from a specialized creel room is mated to rubber from the processing mills to create wide, flat sheets that are cut to size and moved to the tire-making machine.

5. The innerliner is a sort of built-in inner tube that begins as a double layer of synthetic gum rubber.

6. The bead is formed on a high-tensile steel backbone, which will eventually fit against the wheel's rim.

Two machines then come into play to combine each of the six components into what is known as a "green" (because of its raw, uncooked state) tire. One machine constructs the carcass from beads, plies, innerliner and sidewalls. The other handles the tread and underlying belts. The two sub-assemblies are then joined and ready for the super-hot, high-pressure mold.

At this point, the green tire does not have its distinctive tread pattern, nor does it look like it will fit on any wheel. Its beads, normally tucked in and ready to be seated against a rim, splay outward. The sidewalls are as blank as fresh copy paper. The transformation to a recognizable high-performance or truck or winter tire will take place in the curing press.

Vulcanization, the magic process to which Charles Goodyear devoted his life, occurs under heat and pressure in a multi-piece mold, which is also where the tread pattern and sidewall writing are impressed. Not only does the mold push inward against the green tire—like a waffle iron presses against batter—but a rubber bladder capable of exerting extremely high pressure forces the inside of the tire against the mold. The curing process subjects the green tire to 300 degrees for anywhere from 12 to 25 minutes depending on size—or about as much cooking time as the average frozen thin-crust pizza requires.

Released from the mold, tires travel by conveyor belt to quality control personnel who inspect each unit by hand and by eye. Any rubber flash from the mold will be removed at this point, and some tires will be spot checked by X-ray or by dissection to ensure a perfect batch.

If any blemishes or problems are found, the tires are rejected and recycled. Some companies will sell tires with blemishes that are cosmetic in nature and don't affect performance or safety, but only after labeling them as such.

The mold is the final step in forming a radial tire. It's the mold's inner surface that shapes the tire's tread design. The distinctive Aquatred pattern was a real departure from conventional tread layout when it was introduced. Today such radical designs are quite common. (Photo Goodyear)

Because the tread is the only true "signature" of a tire, manufacturers have used show cars to display some wild tire design concepts. These crazy treads from Goodyear have appeared recently on the (from upper left to bottom right) Dodge Avenger, Chrysler Kahuna, Chrysler Tomahawk, Ford 427, Ford Freestyle, and Ford Model U. (Photos Goodyear)

These Goodyear Eagles have passed inspection and are headed for shipping. (Photo Goodyear)

Getting information from a sidewall can be an exercise in frustration if you don't know how to decode the "tire-oglyphic" symbols. The charts and explanations in this section will turn a confusing donut of curved black-on-black print into an open book.

Be aware that while sidewall information has become somewhat standardized, there are still variations from manufacturer to manufacturer and country to country. The following information covers the most widely used formats for passenger cars and light-duty trucks.

MANUFACTURER

Example: Goodyear

It might seem minor to point out something as obvious as the manufacturer's name on the sidewall. After all, it will likely be the largest and most legible portion of text on the tire. The manufacturer's name is important, however, because it is a good idea to give weight to a company's reputation when purchasing such a critical component of automotive safety equipment.

Before spending hard-earned dollars on a set of tires, ask yourself if paying a little bit extra for a top brand will buy peace of mind. Does this tire maker have a reputation for quality products? Have any of your friends had good luck with tires from this company? What sort of recalls has this manufacturer experienced in the past?

MODEL

Example: Aquatred

Model names are transient with most tire companies. The high-performance tire of last year is now a label that runs through the touring and generic passenger car lines.

With specialized models running the gamut from run-flat ultra-performance tires to Severe Snow applications and everything in between, it can take quite a bit of research make a decision. Visit a company's Web site to get the latest information about what models are right for your needs.

Product testing and development continually improve the tires you buy. (Photo Goodyear)

Aquatred is
the model name
of this tire.
(Photo Goodyear)

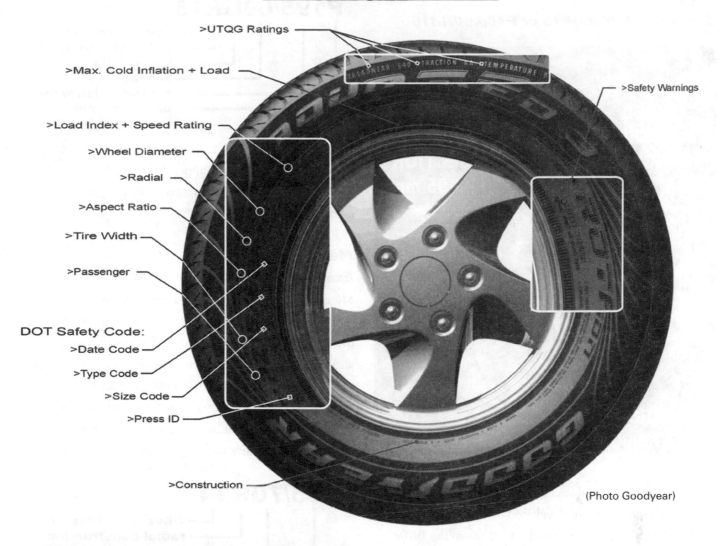

>UTQG Ratings

>Max. Cold Inflation + Load

>Load Index + Speed Rating

>Wheel Diameter

>Radial

>Aspect Ratio

>Tire Width

>Passenger

DOT Safety Code:
>Date Code
>Type Code
>Size Code
>Press ID

>Construction

>Safety Warnings

(Photo Goodyear)

Every tire sold in this country displays the product's size on the sidewall. (Photo Brad Bowling)

Tires legal for sale in the U.S. must meet size standards established by organizations such as the European Tire and Rim Technical Organization (ETRTO) or America's Tire and Rim Association (T&RA) concerning bead shape, width, diameter, and other parameters. They must also meet Department of Transportation (DOT) standards— passage of which is indicated by a specific "DOT" stamp in the sidewall.

Despite efforts over the last few decades to standardize sidewall information, a tire shopper is likely to encounter one of 10 accepted size labeling systems depending on the product's country of manufacture, purpose (passenger car or light-duty truck), and vintage. This section will address the most common.

P-Metric
Example: P195/60R15 or P195/60HR15

(Photo Goodyear)

P-metric tire sizes always begin with the letter "P" (for passenger) and were developed by the T&RA. P-metric measuring appeared in the U.S. late in the 1970s. The load capacity of a P-metric tire (which appears immediately after the size—see "Service Description" below) is determined by an engineering formula that considers the tire's capacity for and density of air. Since this measuring system includes carefully calculated load rates, it aids new car manufacturers because vehicles can be designed around existing tire lines. Most tires produced in North America are rated with this system.

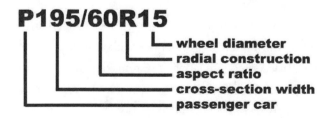

P195/60R15
- wheel diameter
- radial construction
- aspect ratio
- cross-section width
- passenger car

P195/60HR15
- wheel diameter
- radial construction
- speed rating
- aspect ratio
- cross-section width
- passenger car

Additional information appended to the tire's size includes XL, which indicates it has been designed with extra load-carrying capacity.

Metric
Example: 185/70R14 or 185R14

Metric, or European metric, sizing is very easy to read once you've mastered P-metric. Developed in the 1960s by the ETRTO, the only significant difference between metric and P-metric is that the former does not take into account the vehicle's load capacity. A P-metric tire can be substituted for a European metric tire—and vice versa—in axle pairs or sets of four as long as the dimensions, performance category, and speed rating are the same.

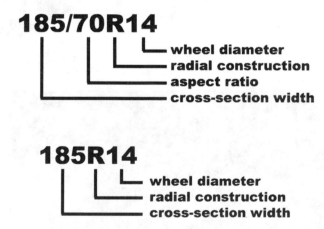

185/70R14
- wheel diameter
- radial construction
- aspect ratio
- cross-section width

185R14
- wheel diameter
- radial construction
- cross-section width

Numeric
Example: 6.95-14

Numeric sizing is, fortunately, no longer practiced in the tire industry. Only reproductions of vintage tires still labor under this archaic and uninformative measuring system. It was created at a time when all tires, no matter the application, were very tall, very skinny, and destined to be mated with a similarly undernourished wheel. For many years following World War II, a tire's sidewall-to-width (otherwise known as "aspect") ratio was either 90 or 80, depending on the time period. Tire widths ranged from 3.5 to 5.5 inches on rims measuring 13 to 15 inches in diameter.

Today, with the ready availability of 35-profile tires on 24-inch wheels, the details of numeric sizing will be of interest only to restorers or owners of cars built before 1970. Whether the intent is to buy exact reproductions of vintage tires for an older car or to mount modern-sized rubber on stock wheels, it is a good idea to be acquainted with the dirt-simple numeric system.

This BFGoodrich Silvertown is a reproduction. It is the stock 6.95-14 size for a 1967 Mustang. (Photo Brad Bowling)

The example offered, 6.95-14, indicates the tire is 6.95 inches through its cross section and designed for a 14-inch wheel. This was a popular tire size in the '60s and it has a close equivalent in today's P-metric system. Multiplying the width of 6.95 inches by a constant of 25.4 converts to 176.53 millimeters in the metric system. The closest modern tire size in a 75-profile tire for a 14-inch rim is a P185/75R14. Switching to such a tire would give a nearly identical overall diameter (new, 25.0 inches; old, 25.3) and section width (new, 7.2 inches; old, 7.0). Such a move increases the load capacity by five percent and gives the buyer the benefit of a modern radial ride.

6.95-14
— wheel diameter
— cross-section width

It is a testament to the last 30 years of technology that this very tire was once standard equipment on the fastest Mustangs Ford produced in the '60s, but equivalent sizes today can only be found on the lowliest of economy cars.

Alphanumeric
Example: F60-15

Introduced in the late 1960s, alphanumeric sizing added information about the tire's load-carrying capacity and radial construction (if applicable), but dropped any reference to the width. The letters A through N—skipping I and M—indicated load; aspect ratio was represented by 50, 60, 70, or 78; an "R" denoted radial plies; and the final number referred to the rim size.

This F70-14 Goodyear Polyglas was a popular size for musclecars in the late '60s. (Photo Brad Bowling)

Conversion from an alphanumeric tire to a same-size P-metric is somewhat trickier than working with the numeric system. The chart on p. 24, compiled by The Tire Rack, gives easy answers to conversion questions by chronologically laying out the various passenger car tire sizing systems.

F60-15
— wheel diameter
— aspect ratio
— load rating

In our example, a 15-inch, 60-series tire with an F load rating (a common musclecar combination in the late '60s) would require a P235/60R15 to maintain an equivalent overall diameter (new, 26.1 inches; old, 25.9) and section width (new, 9.5; old, 9.2).

Be aware the conversion figures do not guarantee a proper fit; fender clearance, suspension components, and wheel size and construction are factors to be considered as well.

Passenger Car Tire Size Conversion Chart

1949-64 NUMERIC "90" to "80"-series	1965-70 NUMERIC	1970-80 ALPHANUMERIC– 78- to 50-series	EUROMETRIC	P-METRIC "82"-series	1980-present EUROMETRIC OR P-METRIC 70-series	65-series	60-series	50-series
			145R13					
			155R13	P155/80R13	175/70R13		195/60R13	215/50R13
5.60-13	6.00-13	A	165R13	P165/80R13	185/70R13		205/60R13	
	6.50-13	B	175R13	P175/80R13				
		C		P185/80R13				
	7.00-13	D	185R13					
			195R13					
						175/65R14		
6.00-14	6.45-14		155R14		175/70R14	185/65R14		
		B	165R14	P175/75R14	185/70R14	195/65R14	205/60R14	
6.50-14	6.95-14	C	175R14	P185/75R14	195/70R14		215/60R14	
		D						
7.00-14	7.35-14	E	185R14	P195/75R14	205/70R14		225/60R14	245/50R14
7.50-14	7.75-14	F	195R14	P205/75R14	215/70R14		235/60R14	
8.00-14	8.25-14	G	205R14	P215/75R14	225/70R14		245/60R14	265/50R14
8.50-14	8.55-14	H	215R14	P225/75R14				
9.00-14		J	225R14					
9.50-14		L						
	5.60-15	A	155R15	P155/80R15		185/65R15	195/60R15	
6.00-15		B	165R15	P165/80R15	185/70R15	195/65R15	205/60R15	225/50R15
6.50-15	6.85-15	C	175R15		195/70R15	205/65R15	215/60R15	
		D						
	7.35-15	E	185R15	P195/75R15	205/70R15	215/65R15	225/60R15	
6.70-15	7.75-15	F	195R15	P205/75R15	215/70R15		235/60R15	
	8.15-15							
7.10-15		G	205R15	P215/75R15	225/70R15	235/65R15	245/60R15	265/50R15
	8.25-15							
	8.45-15							
7.60-15		H	215R15	P225/75R15	235/70R15		255/60R15	275/50R15
	8.55-15							
8.00-15	8.85-15	J	225R15	P225/75R15	235/70R15		255/60R15	275/50R15
8.20-15	9.00-15	K						
	9.15-15	L	235R15	P235/75R15	255/70R15		275/60R15	295/50R15
		N						305/50R15

No matter the car, space saver spare tires are designed for function only, usually on plain steel rims. (Photo Brad Bowling)

Temporary Spare
Example: T115/70D15

T115/70D15
- wheel diameter
- ply construction
- aspect ratio
- cross-section width
- temporary spare

The temporary, or "space saver," spare tire has made its way into millions of trunks since its inception in the late '60s. As cars have become smaller and lighter in the interest of increased fuel economy, manufacturers have all but eliminated full-size spare tires—thus shaving a few pounds from the vehicle's overall weight and reclaiming room for a larger trunk or gas tank.

The most overlooked part of any car is the space saver spare. Just like the other four, it is a pneumatic design and requires air pressure to do its job. This spare should have 60 pounds per square inch at all times. (Photo Brad Bowling)

When new, temporary spares generally contain written guidelines about their intended use somewhere on a label attached to the wheel or in close proximity to the spare tire storage area. Manufacturers recommend driving on temporaries as short a distance as possible and at a slower-than-usual speed. Not only do temporaries not have the same handling, wear, weather, and temperature characteristics as their full-size counterparts, but they often are shorter in overall diameter. Most temporary spares are N-rated tires, meaning their recommended top speed is no greater than 87 miles an hour.

Although this space saver is from a 260-horsepower Mustang GT with Z-rated Goodyears, it is only M-rated (80 mph) and carries a load index of only 96 (1,565 pounds). (Photo Brad Bowling)

Should promoters of various run-flat technologies have their way (see Chapter 3 in this book), even the temporary spare may soon join brass headlamps and stand-alone radiator caps in the automotive history museum. Certain high-dollar sports cars already have exchanged run-flats for spares, and it seems only a matter of a few more years before passenger cars follow that lead.

This comparison photo shows why low speeds are recommended when driving on temporary spares. (Photo Brad Bowling)

Until such time as they become extinct, however, the easiest way to positively identify a temporary spare is by the T that precedes the regular metric numbering system. In our example, the D indicates diagonal (or bias) ply.

Light truck – metric
Example: LT285/75R16

Modern tires designed for light-truck and SUV all-season highway duty are measured using the same system as that applied to passenger cars, the only difference being an LT prefix in place of the P.

LT285/75R16

- wheel diameter
- radial construction
- aspect ratio
- cross-section width
- light truck

(Photo Interco)

31x10.50R15LT

- light truck
- wheel diameter
- radial construction
- cross-section width
- overall diameter

(Photo BFGoodrich)

Light truck – flotation
Example: 31x10.50R15LT

Folks who never embraced the metric system will find the light truck flotation tire measuring format the easiest of all because this chain of numbers is in inches! The first number—31 in our example—tells the tire shopper the overall diameter of the tire in inches when mounted and properly inflated. Next is the cross section width; in this case, the tire is 10.5 inches wide. Ply construction is indicated next—"R" for radial—followed by wheel size and LT to indicate a light truck application.

Conversion from a flotation-type measuring system to a same-diameter LT-metric is aided by the chart on p.27, which lays out and compares the various formats. Supplied by The Tire Rack, it provides easy answers to conversion questions for most popular applications.

Be aware the conversion figures do not guarantee a proper fit; fender clearance, suspension components, and wheel size and construction are factors to be considered as well.

Light Truck Tire Size Conversion Chart

Diam.	75-series +	70-/65-series	60-series -	85-series	75-series -	Flotation	Numeric
34.5						35x12.50R15LT	
33.5				LT255/85R16			
33.0					LT285/75R16		
32.5						33x12.50R16.5LT 33x12.50R15LT	
31.5		P275/70R16		LT235/85R16	LT265/75R16	32x11.50R15LT	7.50R16
30.5	P265/75R15	265/70R16	285/60R17	LT215/85R16	LT285/60R17 LT245/75R16	31x10.50R16.5LT 31x11.50R15LT	9.50R16.5LT
30.0		P255/70R16	P275/60R17				
29.5		P245/70R16	265/60R17		LT225/75R16		8.75R16.5LT 8.75R16.5LT
29.0	205R16 205/80R16 P235/75R15	255/65R16 P235/70R16 P255/70R15	255/55R18		LT235/75R15		
28.5	P225/74R15	P225/70R16 P245/70R15			LT225/75R15	29x9.50R15LT	8.00R16.5LT
28.0			P255/55R17 P275/60R15				
27.5	P215/75R15	P225/70R15			LT215/75R15		
27.0	P205/74R15	P215/65R16	255/5017 P305/50R15 P255/60R15		LT205/75R15		
26.5	P195/75R15	P225/70R14	P295/50R15 P245/60R15		LT195/75R15	27x8.50R14LT	
26.0	P205/75R14 185R14	P215/65R15 P215/70R14	P235/60R15				
25.5	P195/75R14	P205/70R14	P225/60R15				

SERVICE DESCRIPTION

Example: 92H

The service description indicates the tire's load index (92) and speed rating (H). The load index compares relative load-carrying capabilities as determined through manufacturer testing and computer calculation. Tires produced for the majority of non-commercial passenger automobiles test in an index range between 70 and 110. The chart below decodes load index ratings for car tires sold in the U.S. If memorizing this chart seems an extreme measure for figuring the load capacity of a tire, don't despair—that same information, in decoded form, is located elsewhere on the tire sidewall written out in good old American pounds.

In this example, the load index is 93 and the speed rating is W. (Photo Brad Bowling)

Load Index	Pounds	Load Index	Pounds	Load Index	Pounds	Load Index	Pounds
71	761	81	1,019	91	1,356	101	1,819
72	783	82	1,047	92	1,389	102	1,874
73	805	83	1,074	93	1,433	103	1,929
74	827	84	1,102	94	1,477	104	1,984
75	853	85	1,135	95	1,521	105	2,039
76	882	86	1,168	96	1,565	106	2,094
77	908	87	1,201	97	1,609	107	2,149
78	937	88	1,235	98	1,653	108	2,205
79	963	89	1,279	99	1,709	109	2,271
80	993	90	1,323	100	1,764	110	2,337

For light truck tires, this equivalent information is found in the alphabetical <u>load range</u>, which is an estimated ply rating. We say "estimated" because manufacturers do not actually count the number of plies that make up the tire, but indicate an equivalent strength based on earlier bias ply tires. This information does not apply to a standard load P-metric tire, which simply has an XL after the size on the sidewall if it was built for extra load capacity. It will only be found on tires marked with the letters LT before the size or flotation tires.

Category	Max. Speed
L	74
M	80
N	86
P	93
Q	99
R	105
S	112

Category	Max. Speed
T	118
U	124
H	130
V	149
W	168
Y	186
Z	149+

Load Range	Ply Rating
A	2
B	4
C	6
D	8
E	10
F	12

Load Range	Ply Rating
G	14
H	16
J	18
L	20
M	22
N	24

The speed rating, by way of an alphabetical code, indicates the manufacturer's calculated and tested speed at which the tire can carry a load corresponding to its load index. On original equipment applications, it is required that tire speed ratings exceed the maximum speed capability of the vehicle for which they are intended. This is a good rule to follow for purchasing aftermarket tires as well.

Every tire producer's legal department is quick to point out that speed and load ratings only apply to tires that have not been damaged, punctured, repaired, or otherwise modified. Tests are based on carefully controlled laboratory conditions, with mounted, properly inflated tires being pressed against a large-diameter metal drum (to simulate loaded driving conditions).

Speed rating codes for Department of Transportation-approved tires were developed by a European standard. They were originally tested to round numbers in kilometers per hour and then converted to our miles-per-hour system; this explains why the speed break-outs usually do not fall on the 10. Laboratory tests are conducted with properly mounted rims pressing against a large-diameter steel drum revolving at various speeds with a simulated full weight load.

This system of standards has been tweaked some since its inception. In 1991, the V rating was adjusted to reflect an upgrade from a 130-mph limit to a 149-mph top speed. The lower-rated V tires produced before 1991 have the speed symbol within the tire size; higher-rated Vs find the symbol in the service description.

There seems to be some confusion and overlap among the W, Y, and Z ratings. A few years ago, when Z was added to the ratings chart, it was considered to meet the ultimate performance level for modern cars. Since then, technology and wind tunnel time have combined to create a glorious new realm of ultra-high performance vehicles that can use every bit of a 168- or 186-mph tire's capacity. How far above 149 miles an hour a Z-rated tire is good for is a matter best left to engineers and professional test drivers; if a car manufacturer indicates its product can exceed 149 miles an hour, it is wise to step up to the W or Y.

SERVICE INDICATORS

An "M+S" or "M&S" symbol indicates the tire has met Rubber Manufacturers Association (RMA) guidelines for mud and snow use under normal, all-weather driving conditions and has better winter traction when compared to tires not so stamped. M+S tires generally do not have the deep, blocky tread pattern—and, therefore, are absent the excessive road noise—of those designed for rough, off-road conditions.

Yokohama's Geolandar
is M+S rated.
(Photo Brad Bowling)

A step up from M+S is the Severe Snow Conditions rating, which is indicated by a stylized mountain/snowflake symbol. In order to receive this rating, the RMA requires tires meet performance-based criteria involving tread pattern, construction elements and materials proven to enhance a tire's snow performance above and beyond that of M+S.

Other indicators found on sidewalls include orientation markers for uni-directional and asymmetric tires.

DOT APPROVAL/ SERIAL NUMBERS

Example: DOT NJ HR 2AF 529<

The Department of Transportation information string is its own chapter in the sidewall book. "DOT" means, of course, that the tire was produced in accordance with department regulations and guidelines. "NJ" is a manufacturer's plant identification code (in this instance, for Continental). "HR" is a tire size code number. "2AF" indicates the tire type, although this designation is optional at the decision of the manufacturer. "529" tells us the tire was made in the 52nd week of 1999—a sideways triangle symbol immediately

Every tire has a string of information similar to this from the DOT. (Photo Brad Bowling)

following the date code indicates the decade of the 1990s.

UTQG MARKINGS

Example: Treadwear 320, Traction A, Temperature A

The federal government requires all passenger car tires sold in the United States to have a Uniform Tire Quality

Tire testing (Photo Goodyear)

BFGoodrich
g-Force T/A
KDWs (Photo
BFGoodrich)

Grading (UTQG) label according to treadwear, temperature, and traction. The manufacturers themselves, using government guidelines, conduct tests for these capabilities. Traction and temperature resistance grades are based on specific performance levels set industry-wide, but the treadwear ratings system is established by each manufacturer and must be consistent across the brand's models. Light truck and winter tires are exempt from UTQG labeling.

Tires are tested for treadwear on a 7,200-mile cycle conducted under controlled conditions on a standardized course. At the end of their cycle, tires are measured for wear and the life expectancy is extrapolated to 2/32nds of an inch (also known as "wear-out"). Tires are then assigned a relative number based on those figures, with 100 representing the norm. Anything over 100 has a better-than-average wear rate; anything less wears quicker in normal driving. When comparing tires of similar purpose, this number can be very useful—especially if you don't like buying tires very often. For instance, the touring-oriented Daytona Premium GT, with an 80,000-mile tread life warranty, carries a 620 UTQG treadwear rating. In the same category, a Michelin X One, with the same warranty, is graded 700. Since the manufacturer sets the standard, it is possible for these two example models to be closer or farther apart than what the numbers suggest. By contrast, take a look at the ultra-performance Goodyear Eagle F1, which still manages to pull a respectable 280.

Traction is tested on a rough, wet surface decelerating under load from 40 miles an hour. This standard measures a tire compound's traction capability more than the effectiveness of its tread pattern. It should be noted that the traction rating does not reflect the tire's performance handling characteristics or ability to resist hydroplaning. Grades are limited to AA (the best, introduced in 1997), A, B, and C. With established brands, it is seldom the case that a B- or C-rated passenger car tire makes it to market. It is common to find AAs at the top end of the price range, such as the Sumitomo HTRZ II and HTR+.

A tire's resistance to the heat generated by running at high speed and its ability to dissipate that heat are graded with an A (highest), B, or C. Heat tests are conducted indoors in a lab. This rating is especially important because excessive heat can degrade the rubber compound and weaken the tire, leading to premature failure. A grade of C is given to a tire that only meets the minimum requirements; A and B indicate a tire exceeds the guidelines. Most ultra-high performance tires, such as BFGoodrich's g-Force T/A KDW, score an A on temperature testing.

MAXIMUM PRESSURE AND LOAD

Example: MAX. LOAD 670 kg (1174 LBS.) @ 350 kPa (51 PSI) MAX PRESS.

All tires are marked with weight and pressure maximums clearly indicated on the sidewall. Metric readings are in kilograms for load and kilopascals for pressure; English standards use pounds for load and pounds-per-square-inch for pressure.

BALANCE MARKS

Different companies use different marks to reveal "high spot" locations in the tire carcass where plies have overlapped and created a slight imbalance. Dunlop, for example, uses a red dot on its high-performance tires. By matching this point with the "low spot" of the wheel, it will be easier for the installer to cancel out disruptive harmonic vibration through the balancing process. These markings are generally seen on tires installed during the vehicle's production.

WARNINGS

In these litigious times, it's no wonder the bulk of the sidewall word count is taken up by warnings to installers and customers. Most of them refer the reader to other literature available from the company that outlines in more detail safety procedures concerning mounting and use of the tire.

OEM STATUS

As if there weren't enough data stamped on the sidewall, many factory-installed tires feature an Original Equipment Approval Code that denotes the manufacturer for which they were designed. For instance General Motors uses "TPC," BMW is represented by a star symbol and an "N-0" or "N-1" can be seen on tires built specifically for Porsche.

CHAPTER THREE
TYPES OF TIRES

Cars have tires for the same reasons we wear shoes—to gain traction, to prevent damage, and to absorb vibrations and impacts. The most fundamental questions to be asked when making a decision about new tires (or shoes) are: What are they supposed to do and what type do I need?

HIGH-PERFORMANCE AND ULTRA HIGH-PERFORMANCE

Is your car bright red? Does it feature a logo of a prancing horse and the name of an Italian manufacturer?

It's no longer the case that only Ferraris and Porsches require expensive high-performance tires for their vehicles. The speed rating of an OEM tire must meet or exceed the actual top speed of the car on which it's being installed at the factory. Just about every carmaker sells a sports car, coupe, or sedan in the United States that can double the highest state speed limits, so the upper stratosphere of performance rubber is not as rare as one might think.

The BFGoodrich T/A KDW qualifies as an ultra high-performance tire. (Photo FGoodrich)

By definition, an ultra high-performance tire is V- or Z-rated (149 and 149+ mph) or higher with an aspect ratio of 55 or lower. A high-performance tire has a speed rating of

SEEN ON THE STREET

Vehicle:	1990 Nissan 300-ZX Twin Turbo
Owner:	Luke Pavlick
Wheels:	Borbet Type VS 17x8 inches
Tires:	Dunlop SP Winter Sport M2, 235/45VR17 M+S
Handling upgrades:	332-mm Stop Tech brake kit with four-piston calipers, stainless steel lines and cross-drilled rotors

Quote: *"The Twin Turbo came from the factory with a 16x7-inch wheel and 225/50-16 tire on the front and a 16x8-inch wheel on the back wearing a 245/45-16 tire. I changed the size to accommodate my brake upgrades; I wanted to give everything clearance."*

(Photos Brad Bowling)

U (124 mph) or H (130) and an aspect ratio of 60 or lower. They are designed with flat-out, ultimate speed and cornering in mind. Sidewalls are usually quite thin—as low as the 30% to 35% range—which doesn't permit much shock absorption from bumps on the road. In general they are excellent performers in dry conditions, compromised on wet roads, and relatively useless on snow.

Because sports car owners value handling and speed above all else, the tires are designed to be as light as possible so unsprung weight is reduced to improve suspension responsiveness. Great leaps have been made in the engineering that goes into high-performance tires, with many brands benefiting from road course racing technologies that make such products more practical for everyday use.

The downside to tires designed for high speeds and extreme handling is a one-two punch to the wallet. They can be painfully expensive; and they wear faster than other types of tires, which means you have to buy them more often.

To compare apples to apples, let's use a 2001 Honda Civic as an example because it comes standard with very inexpensive but capable tires. The Civic is a popular vehicle with young enthusiasts who like to boost the performance and dress it up like a race car. It is built for economy and to be a pleasant grocery-getter, but in the hands of a youthful driver with disposable income is often upgraded to the highest-rated performance tires and largest wheels possible.

The Tire Rack currently offers a Kumho Touring Plus 732 T-rated (118 mph top speed) tire in the car's stock 195/60R15 size for around $140 a set. The speed range is realistic for the Honda and Kumho indicates a treadwear rating of 400, or four times the norm for this category.

Good practical stuff, like a pair of Chuck Taylor High Top shoes—the kind our hypothetical Civic owner wouldn't be caught dead in, although Dad still thinks they are very "cool."

Returning to The Tire Rack, we see the motivated Civic driver can upgrade to 18-inch wheels and W-rated (168 mph top speed) tires. Yokohama offers a 215/40R18 Parada Spec-2 for $544 a set with a treadwear rating of 300—meaning it has substantially less tread life than the cheaper touring tire.

For the Civic, a move to ultra high-performance tires means a higher replacement bill paid more often during the life of the car.

By comparison, some owners do not have the option of going with a less capable, lower performing tire. Let's say it's time to change tires on a 2002 Chevrolet Corvette, which came stock with 245/45R17s in the front and 275/40R18s in the rear—all V-rated.

If the Corvette owner wants to get by as cheaply as possible, he should consider a set of W-rated ContiExtremeContacts from Continental for $540. On the other extreme, four Y-rated (186 mph) Michelin Pilot Sport A/S Zero Pressure tires in the correct sizes will burn a $1,220 hole in his pocket. Remember, the flip side of high-performance is high cost.

MAX PERFORMANCE

Depending on the manufacturer in question, you may encounter the "max performance" category of tire. These are W-, Y-, or Z-rated tires that use highly advanced materials and technologies to excel at dry and wet handling, such as Goodyear's Eagle F1. In general, though, all ultra high-performance and max performance tires fall under the heading of high-performance.

Available in W- or V-rated versions, the BFGoodrich Scorcher T/A is a high-performance tire. (Photo BFGoodrich)

Falken's FK451 falls in the max performance category. (Photo Falken)

PERFORMANCE ALL-SEASON

Any tire that fits the criteria of the three categories listed above but compromises ultimate handling for some wet and cold weather capabilities is considered a performance all-season product.

Dunlop's SP Sport 5000 is a performance all-season tire. (Photo Dunlop)

TOURING

Touring tires place a strong emphasis on a comfortable, quiet ride with a long tread life, but without entirely sacrificing performance. This is generally the category most people shop when they are looking to replace rubber that came on their family sedan from the factory. Typically, they run from 60- to 70-profile, carry speed ratings in the S, T, H, or V range and have mud and snow (M+S) capability.

Bridgestone Turanza LS-T touring tire (Photo Tire Rack)

GRAND TOURING

Grand touring focuses more on performance aspects and offers slightly less of the quiet, refined ride of a touring tire with some sacrifice of tread life. Aggressive tread patterns give them the appearance of high-performance tires. Generally rated for M+S, the grand touring category is home to the 50- through 65-profile tires with speed ratings of H, V, and Z.

Kumho's ECSTA KH-11 is a very capable grand touring tire. (Photo Tire Rack)

GRAND TOURING ALL-SEASON

Combining the high-speed capabilities of a performance tire with the long tread life of a touring tire and all-weather utility creates a grand touring all-season tire. Automakers prefer grand touring all-season tires as OEM rubber because of their all-around capable nature. They fall in the same profile and speed range of the grand touring models, and are also designed for mud and snow traction.

ALL-SEASON

This is what you ask for when you have a passenger car and want a bare-bones, inexpensive tire—the only frill at the bottom of the pile being a mud and snow rating. Generally rated for speeds on the low side of the scale in the S and T range, all-season tires are engineered for a quiet ride, long tread life, and a low purchase price.

Every tire manufacturer produces one or more of these bread-and-butter lines, usually with confidence-inspiring names such as Integrity (Goodyear), Harmony (Michelin),

Control (BFGoodrich) and Affinity (Firestone), to name a few. Prices per tire are very attractive in this category; a recent scan of online tire distributors showed a range of $32 to $82 per tire for a hypothetical 2000 Chevrolet Cavalier wearing a 195/70R14.

If race car-like handling is not your top priority when buying tires, there is good value to be found among the all-seasons; Goodyear's Aquatred 3 and Uniroyal Tiger Paw with flat-preventing NailGard sit smack in the middle of the category's price range.

Uniroyal's Tiger Paw with NailGard is a reasonably priced choice for an all-season tire. (Photo Uniroyal)

WINTER

The advance of technology has given us a variety of cold-weather rubber from which to choose. There are performance winter tires, which are available as direct replacements for OEM tires in H or V speed ratings. Since they are not as capable as traditional, no-compromise snow tires they are recommended for people who only occasionally encounter snow-covered roads in the winter and want to maintain their sporty car's handling ability year round.

What people normally think of as winter rubber are the studless ice and snow tires. Seen frequently in areas of the country that stay blanketed under snow for months at a time, studless tires sacrifice some dry weather handling ability for mobility under the worst of traction conditions. Since snowy roads are not normally driven at excessively high speeds—and because the rubber compound's

temperature range is engineered to work best in extremely cold environments—this type of tire only receives a Q rating (99 mph top speed).

Studdable winter tires combine an aggressive tread design similar to regular ice and snow tires with the ability to add metal studs for ultimate traction on snow and ice. Since many states have banned the use of studded tires due to the damaging effect they have on asphalt, owners often get by without taking advantage of that feature.

The downside to winter tires really only applies to warmer times of the year, when their noisier tread and stiffer compounds make them seem less than ideal. For that reason, snow belters are accustomed to having 2 sets of wheels—one mounted with "summer" tires and the other with winter tires.

Before the advent of the low-profile performance winter model, all snow tires were designed with fairly tall sidewalls because a long, narrow footprint pushes through the white stuff more effectively than one that is short and wide. Traditionally, people would "downsize" their winter tires to get a narrower section width and taller section height, often dropping an inch or so in wheel diameter. Because automakers today are equipping sports cars and sports sedans with bigger brake components and other tightly configured equipment, it is not always possible to "downgrade" the wheel size in order to get a traditional studless tire on the vehicle, which explains the popularity of the performance winter tire.

To illustrate an example of downsizing for performance winter tires, let's take a 1997 Audi A4 Turbo Quattro, which still wears its optional OEM-size 205/55R16 high-performance radials during the warm months. Because the owner is a conservative driver and does not imagine himself a world rally champion every time he finds a snowy stretch of road, he decides to revert the Audi to its base model tire and wheel size—195/65R15—for winter. Since he wants to keep his good alloy rims away from the road salt, he'll be buying some inexpensive steel wheels to use during snow season, and he knows that smaller tires tend to be cheaper than larger ones when compared model to model. Our example owner uses the car's base model tire size (usually located on a label on the driver's door or under the hood) because he knows the manufacturer could not install that smaller tire if it did not have an adequate load rating for his model.

His shopping turns up a deal on a set of Dunlop Winter Sport M2s in his size and a set of black steel wheels for around $500. He can find a set of cheap hubcaps for another $50 and put those good performance tires away for a long winter's nap.

Running shoes and loafers feel great on your feet when it's warm out and the ground is dry, but when the white stuff hits the ground, it's time to switch to snow boots. The same is true for your car. Why slide around on high-performance tires designed for warmer operating temperatures when there are such good winter tires to be had? (Photo Brad Bowling)

Do you have a stack of mounted Bridgestone Blizzaks or other winter tires sitting in your basement, attic, or closet? It's not only a good idea for your winter driving safety, but it saves wear on your good summer tires. (Photo Tire Rack)

A Goodyear engineer tests cold-weather characteristics of the Ultra Grip Ice traction tire inside the Eglin Air Force Base's climatic chamber in Florida. The chamber can reach temperatures as low as negative 65°F—the point at which the rubber parts of a car can become brittle and shatter. (Photo Goodyear)

The Dunlop SP Winter Sport M2 is a good choice for our example winter driver as it retains good performance while maintaining traction in standing snow. (Photo Tire Rack)

VINTAGE

There's never been a better time to be an old car or truck enthusiast than right now. Parts for everything from Model Ts to musclecars can be purchased as reproductions from original molds—often of higher quality than when new thanks to modern materials. This bonanza of new old parts applies to tires as much as it does to weatherstripping, fenders, and big hood ornaments, with dozens of vintage favorites being re-popped every year.

There is not enough volume for a major manufacturer to continue production and marketing of obsolete models, which has opened the door for smaller enterprises to serve the market. For example, Goodyear does not have incentive to start making its '60s-era Polyglas GT alongside its modern Eagle radials. It might sell a few thousand of the Polyglas tires each year compared to millions of Eagles. Companies like Coker Tire in Chattanooga, Tenn., have made arrangements with major producers to buy or license original molds, which then allows them to contract with lower-volume factories to make batches of vintage tires. (Read more about this niche market in the Coker Tire entry in the Tire Brand Directory section of this book.)

The reproduction tire industry as a whole seems to maintain high quality standards because in most cases companies must answer to the original manufacturer. This doesn't mean, however, that there aren't occasionally some shoddy products on the market. For your safety and peace of mind, find out the story behind the vintage tires you are considering. See if any other hobbyists have had experience with that particular company and its products before purchasing.

Large swap meets, catalogs, and the Internet are great ways to find out if a certain vintage model is currently available as a reproduction.

The vintage musclecar crowd, like the owner of this GTO convertible, is usually reluctant to "modernize" its cars with non-stock wheels and tires. This red Goat is wearing its original steel wheels and bias-ply tires. (Photo Brad Bowling)

Among its many vintage tires, Coker reproduces the BFGoodrich Silvertown. (Photo Coker Tire)

In 1998 a landmark was reached in the history of the American auto industry when more light truck models were sold than cars. That's a huge development for a market segment that for decades was easily defined as half-to one-ton pickups and the occasional sport utility vehicle—all vehicles whose rough rides and Spartan interiors were clearly not designed for the soft living of the 21st century. Initially only farmers, construction workers, and forestry personnel had any real need for these big, fuel-thirsty, four-wheel driven machines.

There have been small, but significant, steps toward what today is a full-blown love affair between the public and light trucks:

- **The custom van craze of the late '60s and early '70s**

- **Subaru's focus on all-wheel-drive passenger vehicles in the mid '70s**

- **The introduction of compact pickups from Japan in the late '70s**

- **Chrysler's debut of the minivan in the mid '80s**

- **Establishment of a mid-size pickup/SUV range with Dodge's Dakota in the late '80s**

- **"Crossover" vehicles that are part car/part truck as first seen in the '90s.**

Pickup trucks and SUVs are such a major marketing segment today that tire companies devote much research effort to optimizing ride, handling, and comfort for them. (Photo Goodyear)

America surrendered the large, roomy cars it had enjoyed since
the '50s, like this 1955 Chevrolet Bel Air, and quickly moved into large, roomy SUVs. (Photo Brad Bowling)

A WHEEL BARGAIN

During research for this book we discovered the smartest way to buy wheels and tires is with a car or truck already attached to them. Cruise the used cars lots and let someone else spend the big bucks.

This black 2000 Cadillac Escalade, loaded to the headliner with luxury, was sitting on a local lot with 49,000 miles on the odometer. Its first owner installed a sweet set of 17-inch Niche alloy wheels and 265/70R17 Michelin LTX M/S tires, drove it a while and traded. For an asking price of $26,900, you are practically getting the aftermarket wheels and tires for free. (Photos Brad Bowling)

(Photos Brad Bowling)

Perhaps the most significant factor in the tremendous popularity of trucks and SUVs today was the relaxed Corporate Average Fuel Economy (CAFE), emissions and safety standards those models were assigned in the '70s when compared to traditional cars. That's not to say there aren't federal guidelines that must be met by light trucks—there certainly have been all along—but truck engineers had a much freer hand initially to design and build what was once considered a relatively small-volume, specialized type of transportation.

As America reluctantly gave up its truly huge cars in the name of improved gas mileage and pollution standards, automakers and the auto-buying public began to realize that the door was wide open for production of more Chevrolet Suburbans, Jeep Wagoneers, Ford Broncos, and Dodge Ramchargers. With some suspension tuning to soften the ride, creature comforts (cruise control, adjustable steering wheel and cloth- or leather-covered seats), the requisite power amenities (steering, brakes, and windows) and family-friendlier styling, America happily drove its 15-mpg 4x4s through a canyon-size loophole and onto the public highways.

Essentially, SUVs and all their many variations became the big cars we thought we had lost—just a little higher off the ground. Where once Ford's Country Squire station wagon was the overloaded symbol of family life and vacation, in its place we find the quite roomy Escape, Explorer, Expedition, and Excursion. Recent figures indicate that 34% of SUVs and 71% of pickup trucks are built as two-wheel drives, suggesting that many buyers have no intentions of taking their shiny new vehicles into dirty, low-traction environments any more than they would have driven through mud in the family's Oldsmobile Vista Cruiser station wagon.

Popularity of the SUV has brought with it further development and sales of truck-like products; so many that categorizing the different types, sizes, and purposes is no doubt someone's full-time job in the federal government.

Despite this wide range of vehicles available to consumers under the light truck heading, purchasing tires for them can be conveniently boiled down to a handful of manageable segments as defined by the vehicle manufacturers. These include the pickup truck, sport utility vehicle, cargo van, and passenger van.

Many pickups and SUVs come standard with tires designed for passenger cars. The reason for this is there is less rolling resistance and weight in a regular P-metric tire (compared to a light truck tire), which translates to better gas mileage and handling. Tires designed specifically for light truck duty must take into account the heavier weight of the base vehicle, which is likely to be built on a full-frame platform; the load-carrying capacities of different models, ranging from half- to one-ton; and the need to elevate the truck chassis for greater ground clearance through the use of taller tires.

When choosing P-metric tires for a light truck application, industry standards reduce the tire's estimated and maximum load capacities by 9% to adjust for the different service characteristics and center of gravity of the vehicle. For example, a P235/75R15 tire for a car might be rated at 2,028 pounds, but in light truck applications would be dropped to 1,845 pounds.

Truck tire manufacturers recommend replacing LT-rated factory tires with LT-rated tires; P-size factory tires with P-size factory tires—unless there is a specific goal in making the change.

They also warn against the mistake of mismatching tire and rim sizes. For example, under no circumstances should anyone mount a 16-inch tire on a 16.5-inch wheel or vice versa. Explosive separation can occur while mounting or driving such combinations. Sizes are clearly marked on wheel and tire to prevent this occurrence.

For our purposes of comparing tires offered for sale to the public for use on light trucks, we'll discuss the following categories—each of which can be had in all-season designs: Sport truck; highway; and off-road.

Over the last decade or so, the concept of the "sport truck" has evolved into its own marketing segment. Simply defined, a sport truck is a pickup or SUV, ranging from compact or full-size, that has been modified for improved handling and performance—usually beginning with its wheels and tires and followed with a lowered suspension to bring down the vehicle's center of gravity. When this trend started on the west coast, it initially applied to two-wheel drive trucks and SUVs only, but in recent years many luxury 4x4s have enjoyed the chrome wheel/low-profile tire treatment as well.

Tires in this category tend to be larger versions of car designs, with necessary increased load ratings built in. Their sidewalls are relatively low and tread patterns are chosen for aggressive traction on the street—not the farm.

For example, the owner of a 2001 Chevrolet Tahoe two-wheel-drive SUV plans to replace her factory 245/75R16 tires and 16-inch wheels with some chrome 18-inchers. She likes the low-sidewall look, and she intends to drop the vehicle an inch or two with springs. Her current tires measure 30.4 inches in overall diameter, and a scan through some tire catalogs reveals a V-rated Pirelli Scorpion Zero measuring 285/55R18 and a 30.6-inch overall diameter. As is always recommended, the new tire has a higher or equal load rating (2,535 pounds) than the one it is replacing (2,271 pounds). Since she is adding only 40 millimeters (1.57

inches) of width to the tire's section, a full-size truck should have no problem accommodating her upgrade, but she will verify this with a fitment expert before purchasing her wheels and tires.

In describing the "sport truck all-season" tire section on its Web site, The Tire Rack uses a phrase that would have resulted in laughter not too many years ago: "You want your pickup or sport utility vehicle to be a little bit more of a 'sports' car, yet you need all-season capabilities..." Before the west coast sport truck craze pushed development of more capable designs, this sentence would have been as ridiculous as saying, "You want your dog to sing like Frank Sinatra, yet you need it to dance like Fred Astaire..."

Now, however, year round truck tires with sporting aspirations can be found in popular sizes from many manufacturers. For our example Tahoe, had the owner thrown all-season capability onto her wish list, the V-rated Michelin Pilot LTX 285/55R18 would have done quite nicely. Models in this category have taller shoulders and tread (11/32-inch on our example Michelin) like regular truck tires, but the ribs or blocks are shaped more like

SEEN ON THE STREET

Vehicle:	1997 Dodge Dakota
Owner:	Brian Martin
Wheels:	Enkei RT-S 17x8
Tires:	BFGoodrich g-Force 255/50R17
Handling upgrades:	Dropped suspension 3 inches in front (control arms); dropped 4 inches in rear

Quote: *"I had to cut away the front fender on the inside a little bit—only about an eighth of an inch. It looked fine just sitting still, but as I was driving, I could feel contact. I noticed a small lip on the inside the tire was rubbing against and smoothed it out. Now, there's no problem. With V-8 power, I had to have some good rubber on the back when I got on the gas, and these Goodrich tires have been doing the job for me."*

(Photos Brad Bowling)

those on passenger car tires.

Highway ribs are for truck owners who intend to put a lot of miles on their tires in dry weather, but don't feel the need to chase Corvettes through corners. When compared to a block design, ribs generate less road noise, while maintaining a decent amount of water dispersal. The long, thin ribs do not lend themselves to ultimate handling but do have long tread life. This is your basic truck tire.

The OEM tires on a hypothetical owner's plain white 1999 GMC Sierra 4x4 work truck measured 245/75R16, and it's time to buy new ones. The owner doesn't need anything fancy and has no plans to change wheels—he just wants to replace them with identical sizes and capacities. His dealer sets him up with 4 Firestone Steeltex Radial R4S IIs with an E load rating (equivalent to a 10-ply capability) and an R speed rating. Although buying an all-season radial would have given him a much broader range of models and designs to choose from, our owner knows that driving in his part of the country never requires all-weather capability.

If the owner of, say, a 2002 Dodge Ram 1500 regular cab two-wheel drive truck wants to replace his factory, base-model 245/70R17s with some highway rib all-season tires in the same size, a set of Michelin LTX A/S rubber will send him on his merry way. Available in D (equivalent to an 8-ply capability) or E load ratings and R and S speed ratings, the Michelins—like most in this category—promise high mileage, low noise levels, and all-season

traction including light snow mobility.

Off-road all-terrain tires are designed for maximum bite and resistance to puncture. Taller, more aggressive tread blocks range from 13- to 18/32-inch in height. Compounds are stiffer to prevent chipping or shredding of the tire against rugged surfaces. Although technology has improved the all-around characteristics of this segment, handling on pavement, noise and smoothness of ride suffer when compared to a good highway rib or passenger car tire. As the name implies, they are most capable in dirt or gravel.

All the major tire manufacturers have models for this application. For an example, let's take a very popular truck model, the Toyota Tacoma 4x4, which for 2003 came standard with 225/75R15s. If an owner were to upgrade with aftermarket 16-inch wheels, he could put on a 265/70R16 tire with little concern for clearance or fitment. The Bridgestone Dueler A/T D693 in that size has a standard load rating and a speed rating of S. Yokohama also offers a Geolandar A/T Plus II in this size.

Off-road maximum-traction tires are for drivers who are most likely to get stuck, but don't want to be. Characteristic of this category are deep blocks of tread that extend all the way past the shoulder and partially down the sidewall. These are the tires that most sacrifice noise levels, dry handling, and comfort for traction, although the latest examples are more practical for year round use than their predecessors.

Looking up off-road maximum-traction tires to fit a

Don't ever try this in a car you are still paying for! This Class 3 Ford Bronco in the SCORE International Off-Road Racing series spends half its time in the air and the other half on blistering sand and jagged rocks. Its off-road all-terrain rubber soaks up abuse that your street tires should never encounter. (Photo BFGoodrich)

The BFGoodrich Krawler T/A exhibits the aggressive characteristics of an off-road all-terrain tire. (Photo BFGoodrich)

There are tires made just for people who, above all else, do not want to get stuck. This Super Swamper TSL Bogger is just such a tire. (Photo Interco)

1988 Ford Bronco wearing 235/75R15s reveals quite a variety of choices. Kumho's Venture MT has a speed rating of Q. Goodyear's Wrangler MT/R has a load rating of C and a speed rating of Q.

LOSE THAT SPARE TIRE

Statistics tell us that the average person experiences a flat tire every 3.9 years. What part of town will you be in at what time of day when your 3.9 years are up? There is never a convenient time to have a flat, but there are certainly some dangerous ones. In the early days of the automobile, it was common for a car traveling any distance to carry several spare tires and an extensive tool kit for making roadside repairs. Blowouts were common due to primitive materials and engineering, making such equipment essential.

Today, most cars are equipped with a space-saver—a

If you don't like digging the spare tire out of the trunk at 2 a.m. in the rain, consider one of the many "extended mobility" options available. Some are very inexpensive. (Photo Brad Bowling)

miniature spare tire that is entirely unnecessary while all four road wheels are turning happily along the pavement and tends to be at the very bottom of a stack of 6 suitcases, 2 garment bags, and a baby's collapsible playpen when it is needed.

Anyone whose blood pressure increases thinking about

Full-size spares are seldom seen outside of trucks, SUVs and larger sedans. (Photo Brad Bowling)

the last time this happened is a candidate for one of several systems designed to keep a car safely mobile after a tire has been punctured. So far, no tire has been designed that can remain intact against all possible road hazards, but adding more years to the 3.9 until your next unplanned roadside stop could be a reward just for reading the next few paragraphs.

If your car has one of the following systems, it is <u>not</u>

recommended you reclaim extra trunk storage by leaving the spare tire in the attic. Some states include a working spare on their list of mandatory safety equipment to be inspected along with horns, headlights, and turn signals.

Tires with built-in sealant layers

The simplest, oldest, and least expensive way to "enhance mobility" after punctures is through a self-sealing layer sandwiched between the tire's inner liner and outer tread. Such products have been sold for more than 20 years, with ever-improving results, but with a 10% to 25% increase in cost over a brand's non-sealing counterpart, most aftermarket consumers consider the self-sealing tire a costly and unnecessary extravagance.

Early versions of this idea sometimes suffered from a sealing layer that migrated to low spots in the tire, causing chronic balancing problems. Uniroyal was the first to offer a new generation of tires designed around advanced self-sealing technologies and a purpose-specific all-season carcass. Its Nailgard system is available on passenger cars and minivans in its Tiger Paw model and for SUVs and trucks in its Laredo tires.

Uniroyal claims that its Nailgard seals up to 90% of

Uniroyal's Tiger Paw with Nailgard. (Photo Tire Rack)

punctures to the tread up to a size of 3/16-inch without any loss of air pressure, although independent controlled tests show an even higher sealant success rate for the product.

Because consumers have historically been reluctant to

pay the extra dollars for a self-sealing tire, let's make a quick online shopping trip to price this safety feature for a 2002 Chevrolet Express van. The Express is a typical vehicle a family might take on vacation in customized form or a contract worker might turn into a mobile tool shed. Either way, its owners do not want to be changing a flat tire on the side of the Interstate.

The Tire Rack currently offers a 235/75R15 Uniroyal Laredo all-season tire for $71 each. The approximate load- and speed-equivalent Laredo with Nailgard goes for $76— a difference of $5, or $20 for a complete set of four. Twenty dollars today doesn't even buy a full tank of gas, but it can buy some peace of mind about being stranded due to a flat tire. It is interesting to note, though, that the bulk of Uniroyal's Nailgard sales are not the general public, but to car manufacturers who offer the feature as part of a safety package from the factory.

Uniroyal claims its puncture seal material works to 30 degrees below zero, and that the weight penalty for the Nailgard option is only a couple of pounds. On a van the size of our example Express, such an increase is minimal and would almost certainly go unnoticed by the driver. The company warns that drivers should have puncturing objects removed from the tire immediately on detection because a nail or screw can work its way around as the vehicle is driven. This could enlarge the hole to the point that the sealant can no longer repair itself.

Firestone has its Sealix system, which has two sealing components pumped directly beneath the tread in a spiral application during manufacture. Although the procedure is slightly different from the Uniroyal product, self-sealing properties are roughly equivalent.

General offers a similar product under the name Gen-Seal.

The run-flats

Serving a similar purpose to the self-sealing technology, but costing the consumer quite a bit more, is the "run-flat" or "self-supporting" design. In principle, developing such a tire was a simple matter of stiffening the sidewall to the point that it could support the weight of one corner of a car. In reality, it required completely rethinking rubber compounds and belt materials in order to produce a run-flat tire whose stiffness would not render it incapable of delivering a smooth ride.

Several companies manufacture tires in this category,

Goodyear has pushed development of its EMT run-flat technology and sells it on everything from the Aquasteel (left) to its OEM Corvette Eagle F1 tire. (Photos Gooyear, Brad Bowling)

with each getting its own catchy name. Goodyear has its EMT (Extended Mobility Tire); Dunlop touts its DSST (Dunlop Self-Supporting Technology); Michelin offers Zero Pressure; Firestone its RFT (Run Flat Tire); Yokohama includes the feature in its AVS (Advanced Vehicle System) but they all work in similar ways. Layers of stiff rubber are sandwiched between two rows of cords in the sidewall, which makes the uninflated tire's exterior only look slightly under-inflated.

Run-flats were conceived as being 100% compatible with standard wheel designs, but all systems require the accompaniment of in-wheel air pressure monitors as neither tire is designed to be run entirely without air except in emergency situations. Manufacturers recommend driving no more than 50 miles at 55 miles per hour before having a qualified technician inspect and repair the tire.

The first mass-produced car to benefit from this technology was the fifth-generation Corvette (a.k.a. C5), which was outfitted with max performance Goodyear EMTs across the board. Shopping for the factory-spec Goodyears reveals why run-flats may not be the runaway hit their makers had hoped. A set of four Y-rated Goodyear Eagle F1 GS tires (245/45R17 front, 275/40R18 rear) currently run $834 in "regular" D3 form and $1,190 as EMTs. That's a 42% difference for a car that already has the mandatory pressure-monitoring equipment. An owner switching a conventional car to fun-flats will also incur the cost of an aftermarket monitoring system—around $250.

This technology was tested and written about by every major auto magazine when introduced, all verifying makers' claims that little comfort and performance were sacrificed for the run-flat capability. With such an engineering marvel in its stable, Goodyear can be forgiven for enthusiastically suggesting that within the decade all of its tires would be run-flat designs. Consumers, even of high-dollar luxury and sport cars, have not warmed to the technology enough to request it.

Auxiliary supported run-flat systems

Like the run-flats currently in production, auxiliary supported systems serve the purpose of increasing low- or no-pressure mobility. Unlike run-flats, they can require specialized wheels and mounting equipment.

PAX is the name of a system currently in limited production in Europe. Michelin and licensees Goodyear,

This cutaway example shows the normally hidden inner ring of Goodyear's PAX system. (Photo Goodyear)

Sumitomo, and Pirelli are all developing PAX-specific products, which include a hard inner wheel attached directly to the inside center of the rim to act as support for the sidewalls should the tire lose air pressure. Alcoa Wheel and Forged Products has been involved from the beginning by creating various asymmetric alloy wheel designs to complement the new system.

The inner wheel is ribbed for stronger construction and is similar to what has been used for several years by the U.S. Army in its Hummers.

Because the inner wheel carries the weight when needed, sidewalls can be designed to flex as easily as today's conventional tires for maximum comfort. The re-configured bead of the tire is mechanically attached to a

PAX-specific rim—similar to a 4x4 bead lock—not held in place by simple air pressure. Such a setup requires technicians and mechanics with specialized equipment and training.

Michelin claims the PAX system offers high-performance handling, zero-pressure safety, and an incredibly low rolling resistance. As on the simpler run-flat tires, pressure-monitoring devices are mandatory. PAX is available, as of this writing, on the Renault Megane in France and Cadillac plans to introduce its XLR roadster with the advanced run-flat system as standard equipment.

Continental, in the meantime, has been working on a similar system that uses conventional wheel designs called the Conti Safety Ring. This concept, which is currently

For consumers who have just gotten the hang of the P-metric measuring system, the all-new PAX sizing will either be a blessing or a curse. This example photo of an Audi concept tire built by Goodyear reads 295-770R560A. Designers of this innovative auxiliary support system have decided to simplify tire measurement by switching entirely to metric. The 295 refers to the tire's section width in millimeters (as it does with P-metric—in this case, 11.61 inches); the 770 indicates the tire's overall diameter in millimeters (or 30.31 inches); the R means it's of radial construction; the 560 is the wheel's diameter in millimeters (22.04 inches in the example); and the A tells us the wheel has un-matching, asymmetric bead diameters to allow easier installation of the tire over the PAX ring. Since the wheel is asymmetric, the indicated diameter of 560 millimeters is for the "primary" or outside bead. (Photo Goodyear)

standard equipment on the gigantic Maybach 57 and 62 ultra-luxury cars, would attach a steel-and-rubber insert to the drop center of the inner rim. It is in limited use on some European market models, with plans to launch in the United States by 2005. Continental expects the SUV segment to pick up this new technology first. It is unclear at the moment which, if any, system the automotive industry will embrace and promote.

SELF-SEALING TIRES

The Tire Rack's South Bend, Ind., headquarters has a full-size road course and skidpad area for tire testing. (Photo Tire Rack)

The Tire Rack team compared the ride comfort and everyday handling abilities of the standard Uniroyal Tiger Paw AWP against its counterpart with Nailgard protection. (Photo Tire Rack)

Perhaps no one outside the manufacturers' engineering departments has more hands-on testing experience with self-sealing rubber than the enthusiasts at The Tire Rack. Their company has access to a large onsite test track that is used year round in dry, wet, and snowy weather as well as an offsite indoor ice rink that doubles as a cold-weather test facility.

The staff recently had an opportunity to torture several brands of self-sealing tires while driving like maniacs in the name of scientific research. (How do we get that job?)

One test was a comparison between two Uniroyal Tiger Paw tires—one with Nailgard and one without—to determine if the safety sealant brought with it any unpleasant compromises in the areas of handling and comfort. A '99 Toyota Camry sedan was outfitted with 205/65R15s of both types over the course of a two-day evaluation.

The only noticeable differences were a slightly heavier steering feel from the Nailgard tires, which delivered a smoother ride over Interstate expansion joints. Both tires received nearly equal ratings for comfort and handling—despite each Nailgard tire being punctured more than 25 times during testing.

Another two-day test saw The Tire Rack staffers running the Camry through a complete course with regular Firestone FT70c W/UNI-T, self-sealing Firestone FT70c W/UNI-T Sealix and self-sealing Uniroyal Tiger Paw Nailgard tires in temperatures that never climbed above the freezing mark. The purpose of this test was to determine how well self-seal technology really works when it's cold enough to keep folks indoors sipping hot chocolate by the fireplace.

Again, the results indicated the products were up to the task and performing as advertised. During this round of testing, each of the self-seal tires was punctured a total of 33 times—with no quantifiable loss of air pressure.

You didn't really think we could have a whole book on round objects without trying to measure and manipulate them mathematically, did you? A tire is, after all, just a circle. It has a radius, diameter, circumference, and area—attributes that affect the way it performs and how sharp it looks on a car. (We do promise that at no time will you be required to know what Pi means or even how to spell it.)

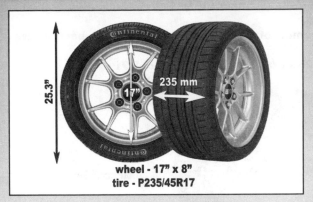

wheel - 17" x 8"
tire - P235/45R17

(Photo Continental)

The formulas on these pages are basic and straightforward (no advanced calculus here) but once mastered will reveal the hidden world of wheel and tire sizing.

All manufacturer-supplied measurements (for 80- to 50-profile tires) are taken from a tire mounted on a "design rim" measuring 70 percent of the section width and filled with the recommended air pressure. Tires are "unloaded" – meaning they do not have weight pushing them against the ground – unless otherwise indicated. Tires with aspect ratios below 50 are measured on a rim that is 85% of the section width.

ASPECT RATIO, SECTION HEIGHT AND WIDTH

Early systems for measuring tires made it simple to figure out section height and width. For example, for many years a 6.50x15 tire measured 6.50 inches in width and roughly the same in height and was mounted on a 15-inch wheel. For any real accuracy, though, it was necessary to consult a tire dealer's fitment chart. Tires of this vintage were designed for cars with very loose specifications for rolling stock.

With today's modern metric and P-metric measuring systems for tires, there is a little more calculating to be done, but it can pay off with greater accuracy. Installing a tire that is out of the manufacturer's specification for size will result in incorrect speedometer and odometer readings. In some cases with modern cars, putting the wrong size wheels and tires on a car can be detrimental to the proper functioning of ABS, traction control, and engine management computer systems.

Example: P225/70R15

CROSS SECTION WIDTH = 225 mm OR 8.9 inches

(Photo General)

Determining section width (the distance between the two sidewalls) is easy if you think in metric terms. In this example, P225/70R15, the "225" indicates the section width is 225 millimeters or 8.9 inches. Here is how to convert from millimeters to inches:

- **number of millimeters x 0.0393701 = number of inches**

- **225 x 0.0393701 = 8.8582725 or 8.9 inches**

(Photo General)

To continue with our example tire, the "70" indicates the aspect ratio or section height in relation to section width—in this case, the sidewall is 70% as tall as the tire is wide. It is necessary to know the section width and aspect ratio in order to calculate the tire's section height. Multiply the section width by the aspect ratio, and your answer is the section height.

- **section width (millimeters) x aspect ratio (percent) = section height**

- **225 x .70 = 157.5 millimeters or 6.20 inches**

Example: 31x10.5R15LT

(Photo Interco)

Buyers of light truck tires measured with the "flotation" system have an easy time determining width in inches, but have to punch the calculator to find section height. For example, a flotation tire labeled 31 x 10.5R15LT has an overall diameter of 31 inches, is 10.5 inches wide and mounts on a 15-inch wheel. To calculate for section height, subtract 15 (the wheel diameter) from 31 (overall diameter) and divide by 2 (because the overall diameter includes 2 sidewalls).

- **(overall diameter – wheel diameter) / 2 = section height**

- **(31 – 15) / 2 = section height**

- **16 / 2 = 8.0 (inches)**

OVERALL DIAMETER

Maintaining the original equipment tire's overall diameter when buying new is critical if you have no plans to spend time at a speedometer recalibration/certification shop or replace the car's rear axle gears.

It is first essential to determine the original tire's diameter—or distance from the ground to the opposite tread face. In the strange, half-metric/half-English world of modern tire measurement, overall diameter is generally given in inches. Begin the calculations by finding the tire's section height in millimeters, then convert to inches.

Example: P245/45R17

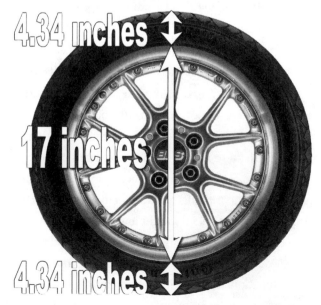

(Photo Continental)

In the example size P245/45R17, the section height is 45% of 245 millimeters, or 110.25 millimeters. Multiplying 110.25 millimeters by the conversion factor 0.0393701 tells us the section height in inches: 4.3405535, rounded to 4.34.

With this information, easy math solves the question of overall diameter. Multiply the section height by 2 (taking into account the 2 sidewalls—one on top, one on bottom) and add the wheel's diameter in inches.

- **(section height x 2) + wheel diameter = overall diameter**

- **(4.34 x 2) + 17 = 25.681107 inches (rounded to 25.7)**

Double-checking the math against tire fitment charts produced by the manufacturers shows Sumitomo, Goodyear, and BFGoodrich all indicate an overall diameter of 25.7 inches for their P245/45R17 tires. Depending on the manufacturer and tire model you are sizing, there may be a slight difference between your calculations and the factory information; anything within 1 percent of variation is acceptable.

The same results will be reached if the following, longer formula is used:

- **[2 x (section width in mm / 25.4) x (aspect ratio % / 100)] + wheel diameter = overall diameter (inches)**

Although all of these dimensions should be considered "nominal"—just like the way one shoe company's size 9 is close to, but not exactly the same as another's—industry standards do make them fairly accurate when compared one brand to another. Section width is allowed a 2% variation, plus or minus, from what is indicated in the tire's stated measurement. Overall diameter is considered accurate to within 0.5% and the rolling circumference may be 1% higher or lower than stated by the factory.

Simply put, "Plus sizing" is a way to increase the diameter of a wheel while decreasing the aspect ratio in order to maintain the same overall diameter and rolling circumference between old and new tires. There are many compelling reasons, especially on computer-controlled modern vehicles, to retain a consistent overall tire diameter throughout the life of the car. As mentioned elsewhere in this book, ABS, cruise control, certain run flat systems, and engine management computers can all suffer in their performance if a wheel's revolutions per mile vary from OEM specs. At the very least, changing a tire's diameter will affect the engine's power band by providing longer or shorter gearing and make the car's speedometer and odometer inaccurate.

*Plus 0

The name might seem to be a contradiction in terms, but Plus 0 should be considered if the goal is to increase the tire's section width for a larger contact patch and improved response without spending a lot of money. A Plus 0 upgrade may or may not be performed with the OEM wheel, depending on the tire manufacturer's recommendation. The "0" refers to the fact that no increase is made in wheel diameter.

205/60R14
(Photo Continental)

PLUS SIZING

14-INCH	15-INCH	16-INCH	17-INCH	18-INCH
	14-INCH PLUS 1	15-INCH PLUS 1	16-INCH PLUS 1	17-INCH PLUS 1
		14-INCH PLUS 2	15-INCH PLUS 2	16-INCH PLUS 2

25.5"
195 mm
25.5"
205 mm
25.7"
225 mm
25.3"
235 mm
25.4"
265 mm

| wheel - 14" x 6" | wheel - 15" x 7" | wheel - 16" x 7.5" | wheel - 17" x 8" | wheel - 18" x 9" |
| tire - P195/75R14 | tire - P205/65R15 | tire - P225/55R16 | tire - P235/45R17 | tire - P265/35R18 |

Example: 195/75R14 to 205/60R14

Our formula reveals that the old tire size of 195/75R14 has an overall diameter of 25.5, and the new 205/70R14 tire measures 25.25—a difference of 0.25 inches.

To review the Plus 0 concept example:

- **Wheel diameter increases 0 inches**

- **Section width increases 10 millimeters**

- **Aspect ratio decreases 5 percentage points**

- **Overall diameter remains the same**

*Plus 1

Under this system, which works across any brand or manufacturer lines, an enthusiast looking for better handling from his car would replace the factory wheels with rims one inch taller.

205/65R15
(Photo
Continental)

225/55R16
(Photo
Continental)

Example: 205/65R15 to 225/55R16

In our example, we are discarding a 15-inch wheel for a "Plus 1" upgrade of 16 inches and looking for a tire with a shorter sidewall to maintain overall diameter. Using the formula explained elsewhere in this chapter, we determine the 15-inch tire has an overall diameter of 25.5 inches, while the new 16-inch setup measures 25.7, which is not a significant variation. Notice the tire's section width grew by 20 millimeters in the process. It is not always the case, but more often than not plus sizing results in a slightly wider tire.

To review the Plus 1 concept example:

- **Wheel diameter increases 1.0 inch**

- **Section width increases 20 millimeters**

- **Aspect ratio decreases 10 percentage points**

- **Overall diameter remains the same**

Plus 1 upgrading is a good step for someone who wants his car to have a different look and feel on the road, but isn't willing to sacrifice ride quality or spend big bucks to get it. The additional 20 millimeters of width is not likely to cause a clearance problem, but all non-stock wheel and tire installations should be visually checked before being driven for the first time, especially if the vehicle has been lowered.

*Plus 2

Plus 2 upgrading is just what it sounds like—essentially a doubling of what we saw with Plus 1.

Example: 205/65R15 to 235/45R17

235/45R17
(Photo
Continental)

The most overlooked part of a wheel and tire upgrade is the speedometer. Any change in overall tire diameter means the speedometer needs calibrating. (Photo Brad Bowling)

Ditching those OEM rims for a set of 17s takes us from an overall diameter of 25.7 inches down to 25.3, a difference of 0.4 inches. Sitting down with a calculator and a tire manufacturer's spec chart produces all sorts of options that work in theory—in other words, they look good on paper, but may not be applicable to certain vehicles. For instance, in the Plus 2 example, whereas the 235/45R17 is 0.4 inches shorter than the OEM tire, a 245/45R17 is 25.7 inches—the same diameter as stock. It may sound great to someone looking to beef up the appearance of his Chevy Cavalier, but the 40 millimeters of extra width may be enough to prevent a proper fit in the wheel well. Tire manufacturers recommend consultation with a fitment expert before spending the money on Plus size upgrades.

To review the Plus 2 concept example:

- **Wheel diameter increases 2.0 inches**
- **Section width increases 30 millimeters**
- **Aspect ratio decreases 20 percentage points**
- **Overall diameter remains the same**

MEASURING SPEEDOMETER ERROR

Many people do not realize how much tire size affects the accuracy of a car's speedometer until they receive their first ticket. The information in this section is useful whether you have changed tire size recently or just suspect your speedometer of giving faulty readings.

There are shops that can calibrate your speedometer, but it's a simple matter to measure with a long stretch of

Interstate highway and a stopwatch. This method works best if the highway does not contain any inclines or declines to affect the vehicle's speed.

Using posted mile markers, time yourself while covering one marked mile at a steady, legal speed (as measured by the speedometer). Divide the number of seconds it takes to drive the mile into 3,600 (the number of seconds in an hour).

- **3,600 / seconds per mile = calculated miles per hour**

Example:

- **3,600 / 60 seconds = 60 calculated miles per hour**

In our example, the driver maintained an indicated 60 miles an hour for one mile, which took exactly 60 seconds. The speedometer is accurate in this case.

Example:

- **3,600 / 65 seconds = 55.4 calculated miles per hour**

A second car covered the same mile at an indicated 60 mph, but took 65 seconds to do it. Some simple math indicates the second car's speedometer is showing 60 miles per hour at a true 55.4 mph. If this error is due to a tire change, it is reasonable to deduce that a lower overall diameter was installed in place of the stock wheels and tires. A taller-than-factory tire will always produce a reading lower than actual speed.

INSTALLING A NON-STOCK SIZE

Now that you've been repeatedly warned against changing the overall diameter of a vehicle's OEM tire, this section deals with ways to manipulate larger- or smaller-than-stock tires to achieve certain goals. It is possible to change the diameter as long as you've done the math.

Although fads and tastes come and go, it is seldom the case that anyone puts smaller tires on a car or truck. The usual scenario is that a car owner looks at his favorite toy sitting in the driveway one day and decides there is way too much air in the wheel wells. Such fits are usually solved by installing springs that lower the body an inch or so, but there is always someone who still wants to stuff as much rubber and aluminum under the fender as possible. With truck owners, the desire to buy bigger and bigger tires seems to start as early as the ride home from the dealership.

Because wheels and tires are really nothing more than the very last gears between the engine and the road, increasing the circumference has the same effect as adding an overdrive to each gear in your transmission. If this sounds like a great idea for your older car or truck that was built without benefit of an engine-relaxing, gas-saving overdrive mechanism, realize that there are consequences for choosing this route.

Whereas a true overdrive gear does not activate until the engine has shifted its way through first, second and third, the "poor man's" overdrive is in play from the second the vehicle begins rolling. The more relaxed overall gearing will most likely increase gas mileage and make for a more relaxed highway ride, but acceleration times will increase as well. In some instances, taller tires may be too much gear for a modest engine to overcome, which can result in pinging and "lugging"—a noisy and damaging condition caused by insufficient torque multiplication.

To illustrate this set of formulas, we will pull from our own experience as a truck owner. Our Ramcharger was built in 1989, the last year Dodge hooked a non-overdrive automatic transmission to its 318 V-8. It was a perfect, boxy two-door SUV but because it was a two-wheel drive truck with the wide body of a 4x4, the stock 235/75R15 tires looked tiny. In order to compensate for the lack of an overdrive as well as beef up the appearance, we had our local tire dealer put a set of 255/75R15s on the factory alloy wheels.

Management of the 318 V-8 was by way of a fairly primitive computer that would not be affected by a change in tire size. It also did not have ABS or any kind of traction control to worry about. Mechanically, all we had to take into account was the effect the upgrade would have on the speedometer.

The decrease in acceleration was not as bad as we had anticipated, but the quieter ride and taller stance were much appreciated.

To quantify how the changes affected the Ramcharger's rear axle ratio of 3.55:1 it is necessary to first solve for old and new tire diameters using formulas we've learned in this chapter.

SEEN ON THE STREET

Vehicle:	1957 Ford
Owners:	Billy and Cammie Moose
Wheels:	Billet Specialties Renegade 15-inch
Tires:	BFGoodrich Radial T/A 235/60-15 front; 295/50-15 rear
Handling upgrades:	lowered suspension; front disc brakes; rear drums from station wagon

Quote: *"With 300 horsepower at the rear wheels, we needed enough rubber that traction wouldn't be a problem. In order to get a foot-wide tire and a deep-dish, negative-offset wheel under the back of the car, we had to shorten the axle by four and a half inches."*

(Photos Brad Bowling)

Example: 235/75R15

- [2 x (235 / 25.4) x (75 / 100)] + 15 = 28.8 inches overall diameter

Example: 255/75-15

- [2 x (255 / 25.4) x (75 / 100)] + 15 = 30.1 inches overall diameter

Subtracting the old tire at 28.8 inches from the new tire at 30.1 inches gives us a net gain of 1.3 inches in overall diameter. Determining how much the Dodge's ground clearance increased is a simple matter of splitting the overall diameter gain in half—0.65 inches.

To continue solving for the "effective drive ratio" and determine what our 3.55:1 rear axle gears "acted" like with the taller tires, use the following formula:

- **effective drive ratio = (old tire diameter / new tire diameter) x rear axle ratio**

- **effective drive ratio = (28.8 / 30.1) x 3.55**

- **effective drive ratio = .957 x 3.55**

- **effective drive ratio = 3.397 or 3.40**

In simple terms, the tall-tired Ramcharger responded to acceleration and cruising as though we had installed a set of rear axle gears with a 3.40:1 ratio. (The closest Mopar gear to this theoretical part is a 3.91:1.) It was enough of a drop to relax the engine at highway speeds but not enough to hurt acceleration. We were too cheap to have the speedometer calibrated for the new tires, so several timed one-mile runs were made to determine the extent of instrument error. It consistently read 10% under calculated speed, so 60 on the gauge was really 66 (60 plus 10% of 60) and 70 was time to talk to the state trooper.

If taller tires are installed for cosmetic reasons only, but you want to retain the vehicle's snappy acceleration, it is necessary to change the gears in the rear axle to compensate. The formula for determining the new gear numbers is almost identical to that for calculating the

effective drive ratio. What you are solving for is the equivalent drive ratio.

- **equivalent drive ratio = (new tire diameter / old tire diameter) x rear axle ratio**

- **equivalent drive ratio = (30.1 / 28.8) x 3.55**

- **equivalent drive ratio = 1.045 x 3.55**

- **equivalent drive ratio = 3.71**

The closest Mopar rear axle gears in this range create a 3.91:1 ratio, which would theoretically give the Ramcharger greater acceleration and take away the relaxed overdrive effect.

USEFUL CONVERSIONS		
TO CONVERT	**TO**	**MULTIPLY BY**
centimeters	feet	0.0328083
centimeters	inches	0.3937008
inches	centimeters	2.54
inches	millimeters	25.4
kilometers	miles	0.6213712
meters	feet	3.2808399
miles	feet	5280
miles	kilometers	1.609344
millimeters	inches	0.0393701
ounces	grams	28.349523
ounces	kilograms	0.0283495
ounces	pounds	0.0625
pounds	kilograms	0.4535924
pounds	ounces	16.0
pounds per sq. in.	kilopascals	6.894757

This 225/35R19 tire Goodyear produced special for the Mitsubishi Tarmac Spyder show car has a 35% aspect ratio—currently the lowest available to the public. (Photo Goodyear)

Perhaps more than any other factor, the aspect ratio determines a tire's handling, comfort, and performance characteristics. It is also the part of a tire's measurement that gets the most attention from the stylin' and high-performance crowds.

The traditional "tall" sidewall with an aspect ratio of 70% to 80%, gives a vehicle a smooth ride because there is much more rubber to absorb shock between the unforgiving wheel and the road. A high aspect ratio (also known as the "profile" or "series") is ideal for luxury cars whose owners are looking for that "riding on a cloud" feeling. High-profile tires continue to be used on light-duty trucks and SUVs that might see off-road use and encounter irregular surfaces and holes.

A high-profile tire's footprint—that all-important contact patch of rubber tread that provides traction—tends to be long but narrow, which is ideal

High-profile tires, like this LT235/85R16 Kumho Road Venture AT, are generally desired by drivers who like a smooth ride for their cars or trucks. (Photo Kumho)

for penetrating a layer of rainwater or snow on the road. It also does wonders to reduce rolling resistance for better gas mileage.

What 70- and 80-profile tires do <u>not</u> do well is turn. Why? Rubber bends; a lot of rubber bends a lot. In a turn, strong forces push against the tire's sidewall as the weight of the car is forced away from the turn by centrifugal force. This conflict between the stiff wheel and the hard ground is handled entirely by the rubber of the sidewall and tread. As the sidewall gives, the already narrow footprint tends to deform, which reduces traction.

Through the late 1960s, tire technology and rubber compounds did not allow manufacturers to design anything with less than an 80% or 78% sidewall-to-section-width ratio. The first 60-series tires were incredibly stiff and available only on high-performance cars such as the fastest Mustang, GTO, Camaro, and Corvette models. The redesigned '69 Mustang, for example, received a last-minute stiffening across the board when it was realized that the Boss 302's Goodyear Polyglas F60-15 tires were harsh enough to damage the chassis.

Development of today's low-profile tires began in the 1970s, with Italian manufacturer Pirelli leading the way.

The lower the sidewall in relation to the section width, the less rubber there is to absorb shock. For some unlucky drivers, this translates to very expensive wheels that must be replaced or repaired after contacting a pothole or other irregularity. It also means a harsher ride for the vehicle's occupants and more noise invading the interior.

The positive side to 50-, 40- and 35-profile tires is that they can greatly increase the handling and braking of a high-performance vehicle. The stiffer sidewall means there is less deflection and deformation in the tread, which keeps the short, wide footprint evenly planted against the asphalt, even under lateral acceleration.

Large-diameter wheels, like this chromed Zenetti P266, are like jewelry for cars. Low-profile tires exaggerate the size of such wheels. (Photo Brad Bowling)

So why the trend toward taller wheels and shorter sidewalls? The performance crowd sees a real benefit to minimizing the amount of rubber it puts between the wheel and the road and is willing to endure a rougher ride and the possibility of rim damage. For the stylin' drivers, minimal rubber means maximum opportunity to show off some expensive aluminum and chrome.

AIR PRESSURE

Because a tire is a pneumatic system designed to support the car's weight and other forms of gravity when in motion, maintaining proper air pressure is vital. While the steel cords of a modern tire give the carcass great tensile strength (meaning you can tug on it all you want, but it's tough to break) it has little compression strength at atmospheric pressure.

When a tire is properly inflated, but has no weight pressing it against the ground, cords pull equally on the bead wire all along the circumference of the tire. Imagine the way a bicycle wheel has individual spokes whose tensile strength pulls the rim toward the hub with equal force. One spoke by itself can probably pull hundreds of pounds without stretching or snapping but when asked to push against a mass immediately bends and deforms.

That same principle of tensile versus compression strength is what's at work in the "skeleton" of a pneumatic tire.

Now, place that inflated tire on the ground with a car pushing down on it and a marvelous, self-supporting system takes over. The cords in the sidewall closest to the ground are relaxed to a degree (as evidenced by the visible bulge), but the air pressure on the top half of the tire is pushing away the bands and cords that run directly opposite from the footprint. The cords on top are pulling up on the bead, lifting the wheel away from the load direction (down).

Driving on tires with insufficient air pressure allows the stiff sidewall cords to bend and straighten and bend and straighten many hundreds of times over the course of a mile. If you've ever repeatedly bent a piece of wire between your hands, you know that the metal becomes hot and eventually fatigues to the point of separation. This is exactly what happens to the cords that support the sidewall if there is not adequate air pressure.

The tread's contact with the road is subject to correct air pressure as well. Engineers estimate that underinflation of 5 pounds per square inch in a high-performance radial tire can reduce tread life by 25%. When you consider that some tires in that category go for $400 to $800 or more a set, spending $50 on a professional-level tire gauge seems like a good investment.

Another important factor concerning proper air pressure comes into play when the tire handles cornering and braking forces. It is pressure from inside the tire that clamps the bead and rim together, preventing the two from separating.

In addition, tires are very effective absorbers of shock and vibration that would otherwise be transmitted from the ground to the wheel and into the passenger compartment. Severe underinflation will weaken the sidewall and allow the wheel to make direct contact with rough pavement. Overinflation, however, can be just as jarring to the ride as too much pressure reduces the sidewall's ability to flex; extreme cases can cause the tire to behave like a solid part of the wheel. A too-stiff tread surface can rip open on contact with a sharp object.

It's easy to determine the correct air pressure for factory-installed tires. It's located in more than one location on a vehicle. This car has it written on a chart in the glove box as well as in the owner's manual. (Photo Brad Bowling)

It is essential to monitor tire pressure on a weekly schedule—before driving the car—in order to avoid the detrimental effects of underinflation. Because radial tires tend to bulge under load, visual inspections are not accurate. Pressure should be checked with a quality gauge. Because even the best rubber is porous on the molecular level, air is constantly leaking through the carcass of a tire—whether it is on a car that is stored or being driven daily—at the rate of 1 to 2 pounds per square inch every month.

Ambient temperature also plays a tremendous role in the air pressure of a tire by as much as a 1 psi decrease for every 10 degrees Fahrenheit dropped. A tire set at 32 psi during the summer when it is 90 degrees outside will likely lose 6 pounds of pressure during the next 6 months, at which point it is very cold outside. A drop to 30 degrees in temperature reduces the summertime pressure another 6 pounds, which means the tire now has only 20 pounds per inch of air pressure, which makes it dangerously underinflated.

Perhaps the cheapest investment a car owner can make

Improper air pressure can overheat and destroy a tire. It looks like this poor guy didn't have a good spare and/or tools when he needed them. (Photo Brad Bowling)

in his tires is to make certain all four valve stems have secure caps in place. Everyday driving exposes the valve stem opening to road grit that can quickly ruin the mechanism and let air flow out.

Engineers design tires of different sizes for a range of vehicles based on a projected load capacity. The capacity cannot be reached if pressure is low, so manufacturers since 1968 have equipped all vehicles with labels indicating the recommended pressure for OEM tires. Some are located on the doorjamb; some are on the rear of the doors; and some are found in the glove box. The same information can be found in most owner's manuals, as well.

Tires designed for extra load capacity (indicated by XL on P-metric tires) only have that added capability if inflated to the proper pressure. For example, a standard load and extra load P234/75R15 might each have a 2,028-pound rating at 35 psi, but the extra load tire increases to 2,183 pounds when pumped to its assigned maximum load

pressure of 41 psi. The standard load tire will not be rated to handle the increased air pressure.

It is not often the case that the vehicle's manufacturer requires the tire's posted maximum inflation pressure. Maximum inflation pressure for a tire is defined as the highest amount of air the chamber is designed to contain when cold—"cold" meaning there is no heat buildup from driving or direct sunlight. If properly inflated and checked under cold conditions, a normal gain of 5 to 6 psi while driving may push the pressure above that posted for maximum inflation, but this does not require letting air out.

The sidewall on this Sumitomo HTRZ II indicates a maximum air pressure of 51 pounds per square inch. (Photo Brad Bowling)

Just like with your teeth—only pay attention to the tires you hope to keep. (Photo Brad Bowling)

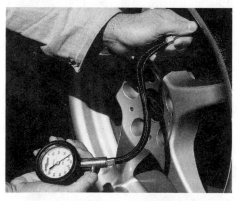

A dial-type or digital pressure gauge is used by professionals because they afford greater accuracy than the pen type. (Photo Brad Bowling)

Doing a scientific study of the effects of ambient temperature on tire pressure would make for an interesting science fair project, if you happen to be a 6th-grader with access to his own indoor rollers and treadmills. Knowing that most middle schoolers don't have such industrial testing equipment handy, our friends at The Tire Rack recently made a serious study of this phenomenon. Here are the results of their experiment.

First, we mounted two tires on wheels. We let them sit overnight to equalize and stabilize their temperatures and pressures. The following morning we set them both to 35 psi. One tire and wheel were placed in the shade while the others were placed directly in the sun. We then monitored the ambient temperatures, tire temperatures, and tire pressures through the day. As the day's temperatures went from 67° to 85° Fahrenheit, the tire that was kept in the shade went from our starting pressure of 35 psi to a high of 36.5 psi. The tire that was placed in the sun and subject to the increase in ambient temperature plus the sun's radiant heat went from our starting pressure of 35 psi to a high of 40 psi. In both cases, if we had set our tire pressures in the afternoon under the conditions of our evaluation, they would have been between 2 and 5 psi low the following morning.

Next, we evaluated the effects of heat generated by the tire's flexing during use. We tried to eliminate the variable conditions we might encounter on the road by conducting this test using our "competition tire heat cycling service" that rolls the tires under load against the machine's rollers to simulate real world driving. We monitored the changes in tire pressure in 5-minute intervals. The test tires were inflated to 15 psi, 20 psi, 25 psi, and 30 psi. Running them all under the same load, the air pressure in all of the tires went up about 1 psi

during every 5 minutes of use for the first 20 minutes of operation. Then the air pressures stabilized, typically gaining no more than 1 psi of additional pressure during the next 20 minutes. This means that even a short drive to inflate your tires will result in tires that will probably be "underinflated" by a few psi the following morning.

Add all of these together, and you can understand why the conditions in which you set your vehicle's tire pressures are almost as important as the fact that you do set it.

It's important to remember that your vehicle's recommended tire pressure is its "cold" tire inflation pressure. It should be checked in the morning before you drive more than a few miles, or rising ambient temperatures or sun's radiant heat affects it.

And by the way, if you live in the North and park in an attached or heated garage you will "lose" pressure when you leave its warmth and venture into the real world outside during winter. Add 1 psi "cold" tire pressure to compensate for each 10° Fahrenheit temperature difference between the temperature in the garage and outside.

—The Tire Rack

On a 25-degree snowy morning the tires on this Subaru Forester have 5 pounds less air pressure than when they were parked the night before and the tires were warm from Interstate driving. Should the owner be concerned? No, this is a normal range for contraction and expansion of air molecules in a tire, as long as they were properly inflated to begin with. (Photo Brad Bowling)

TIRE INFLATION: Exception to the Rule

Although it is not recommended for driving on the street, there is a time when inflating tires above manufacturer's specs might be beneficial. A stiffer sidewall can make a low-slung sports car ride like a potato cart with wooden wheels, but it can greatly improve steering and cornering abilities—up to a point. The only people likely to accept this compromise are motorsports participants, for whom the stiffer carcass and footprint can actually save a tire from self-destruction on the track.

Racing is an exception to the air pressure rule, but follow manufacturers' specs for everyday driving. (Photo Prodrive)

Again, this advice is not recommended for driving on the street. Racers dialing in a new car, suspension, or set of tires—especially amateurs who are budget-limited—generally start off at a certain elevated psi and take practice laps to see how the rubber handles. A chalk mark from the tread to the sidewall is a great indicator for at-speed tire flexing. Adding or bleeding 2 psi at a time can quickly help the driver determine the best pressure for his setup and track conditions.

The Tire Rack, whose high-performance products are bought by a lot of weekend racers, recommends the following ranges for making the conversion from street to track.

Front wheel drive	front	**35-45 psi**
	rear	**30-40 psi**
Front engine/rear drive	front	**35-45 psi**
	rear	**30-40 psi**
Rear engine/rear drive	front	**35-45 psi**
	rear	**35-40 psi**

ALIGNMENT

Before leaving the factory, new cars are set up with optimum suspension and steering alignment specs as determined by the engineers who designed them. Ideally, those components are aligned to provide the vehicle with the least rolling resistance, best straight-line stability, and maximum cornering ability.

That first, perfect alignment begins to suffer as the car ages and as road irregularities take their toll on the chassis and suspension. As settings gradually change, the wheels no longer work in concert to accomplish a trouble-free ride; the first casualties in this conflict are often the tires, most commonly showing excess wear on the inner or outer shoulders of the front pair. Other indications of misalignment include vehicle "crabbing"—that sideways attitude where the rear of the car seems to be trying to pass the front on a straight road—and a strong bias for left- or right-hand curves.

When this happens, and before there is too much irregular wear to save the tire, it is necessary to take the car to an alignment shop. A good alignment technician will test

drive the vehicle before and after the adjustment, check steering linkage pieces for wear or damage before performing the alignment, and inspect the brakes, tires, and power steering pump system to rule out those items as possible trouble spots.

Front-end alignment

The most common type of alignment addresses only the front pair of wheels. It is the least expensive option and will likely even out front tire wear but will probably not solve a serious crabbing problem.

A front-end alignment adjusts settings in three major areas: camber, caster, and toe. To wrap your brain around the fundamentals of these three, think in terms of perspective. Camber must be viewed from the front of the car, caster from the side, and toe from above.

Camber refers to the angle of the wheel when viewed from the front of the vehicle, as measured in degrees, and it has a tremendous amount to do with how a car goes around corners. Zero degrees of camber tells us the wheel is exactly perpendicular to the ground—straight up, in other words.

Negative camber refers to a situation where the top of the wheel is closer to the inside of the vehicle than the bottom. Since the wide stance of a negative camber setup allows a stronger "push" against the pavement during cornering (imagine someone pushing you from the side while your feet are far apart) it's easy to see why most oval-track or road course race car tuners choose it. For the street, engineers dial in a negative camber setting that benefits cornering traction, yet does not tilt the tire so much as to give uneven tread wear when driven in a straight line. Too much negative camber will wear the inside shoulder of the tire faster than the outside.

Postive camber indicates the bottom of the wheel is closer to the inside of the vehicle than the top. With this setup a tire will likely curl under during cornering, causing the sidewall to contact the road surface. Accelerated wear will occur on the outside shoulder as a sign of excess positive camber.

If your car pulls strongly to one side of the road or the other and no wheel, tire, suspension, or steering damage can be found, there is a good chance that the front tires have different camber settings. The vehicle will "favor" the side with the most positive camber. Many front-drive cars do not have adjustments for camber and require a search for worn or damaged parts if an alignment check shows an uneven setting.

Because these camber settings only matter once the car is moving and affected by load and aerodynamic downforce, engineers set alignment specs to anticipate the changes. Traditionally, camber was set between zero and some positive, figuring the weight of passengers and effects of downforce would create an ideal in-motion setting. Today, car makers gain increased stability and improved handling from adjusting camber to slightly negative numbers.

Caster is not generally visible to the naked eye without removing the wheel from the car. The front steering wheels turn on a pivot that is part of the suspension system. The suspension is laid out at a slight angle to the road—in other words, tires are not located directly in line with the upper ball joint and lower ball joint. If the top of the pivot, the upper ball joint, is closer to the rear of the car than the lower point, the caster is positive. If the upper ball joint is ahead of the wheel centerline and lower ball joint, the caster is

negative. Straight-line tracking will be affected by a maladjusted caster setting. With the front tires set unequally, the vehicle will pull to the side with the less positive caster. Excessively negative caster produces light steering and wandering. Excessively positive settings result in a heavy steering feel with strong feedback through the steering wheel on irregular surfaces.

The front wheel of a shopping cart is the best example of a positive caster situation. The wheel is free to move 360° around a pivot line (unlike on your car), but it automatically chooses to follow the pivot line rather than move ahead of it.

Although physics would seem to favor positive caster, most American cars through the mid-1970s were engineered for negative caster for two reasons. First, consumers like the lighter steering effort negative caster produced. Second, at speed and under load the footprint of a bias-ply tire tended to follow the centerline of the wheel due to deflection. When radial tires—which do not experience this type of deflection—became popular and affordable, car makers adjusted the caster and began advertising their products as being "radial engineered." This same adjustment can make a pre-1975 car track better.

Many front-drive cars do not have adjustments for caster and require a search for worn or damaged parts if an alignment check shows an uneven setting.

Toe refers to the difference in distance between the fronts of the tires and the rear of the tires. When the fronts are closer to each other, this is a toe-in condition; when the

rears are closer, it is considered toe-out. Incorrectly adjusted toe can result in a "sawtooth" wear pattern. As with camber, a vehicle's toe settings will change once underway, so specs are dialed in during the alignment that anticipate achieving a zero toe at highway speed.

All cars allow toe adjustment for the front wheels; some are adjustable on the rear as well.

Four-wheel alignment

Each wheel receives a measuring instrument during a four-wheel alignment.

If the vehicle has adjustable rear components, the rear wheel alignment is checked and adjusted first, followed by the front. On vehicles whose rear suspension and axle components do not allow adjustment, the measurements are taken on the rear, but all settings are changed in the front.

DOG TRACK
(uneven axle)

Other factors to check

In addition to camber, caster, and toe, a properly trained technician will use today's modern computer diagnostic tools to check other settings. These include:

- **Steering Center**—means the steering wheel remains centered when the front wheels are pointed straight ahead

- **Thrust Angle**—the direction the rear wheels point; if not aligned with the centerline of the vehicle, it will crab or "dog track"

- **Toe-out on Turns**—in a turn the inside wheel turns sharper by a few degrees than the outside wheel

- **Ride Height**—measured from the rocker panel to the ground; deviation from specs could indicate weakened, ineffective springs

- **Steering Axis Inclination**—from the front of the car at road level, the number of degrees the steering pivot line is away from a true vertical line through the center of the wheel

- **Included Angle**—degrees separating the steering axis inclination and camber line

ROTATING TIRES

About 30 years ago, when everybody in America drove a large rear-wheel drive car powered by a heavy V-8, rotating the four skinny bias-ply tires to get maximum tread life was a simple affair. Your tire shop either used the X or H pattern, and if they were really fancy the full-size spare might get thrown into the mix.

Today's tire rotation chart looks like a football team's winning field strategy. Cars come in front-drive, rear-drive and all-wheel drive with engines mounted who knows where? Some tires feature asymmetric tread; some are unidirectional; some are both. High-performance cars are likely to have different sizes front to rear.

Sometimes it's enough to make a car owner throw up his hands and ask, "Why bother?" Because regular tire rotation can save a lot of money, that's why.

No matter the car in question, the front tires are asked to do an entirely different job than the rears. In all cars, the front tires handle the steering—in most cases with the majority of the car's mass sitting on top of them in the form of an engine. In simplified terms, rear tires are just along for the ride, and much less is demanded of them.

Regardless of which wheels propel your car forward, the front tires need to have the most tread, especially on pavement slick with rain or snow. Bringing a fresh set from the rear every now and then accomplishes this goal.

Tire rotation maintains the handling characteristics of your car from set to set. If you did not rotate your tires, the fronts would wear much quicker than the rears, which changes the balance of traction. Buying a new set would take the car back to the way it drove when new, but handling characteristics would again shift if no rotation is performed over the life of the tires.

Every automobile owner's manual gives recommendations for tire rotation, and tire makers insist on it if the warranty is to be honored. A good rule of thumb is to rotate tires during every oil change—about 3,000 to 5,000 miles for most people. Which rotation pattern you use depends on the vehicle's driven wheels and types of tires.

From the Tire & Rim Association (TRA) come the following 3 approved patterns for rotation. This list applies to non-directional tires with a symmetric tread design.

Figure A

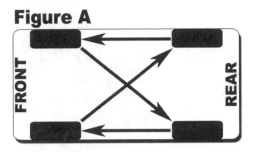

TRA recommends rear- and 4-wheel drive vehicles use the "rearward cross" (Figure A) pattern, where rear tires move directly to the front and front tires move to the opposite rear.

Figure B

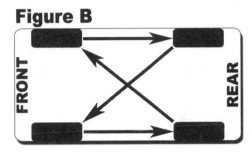

The "forward cross" (Figure B) is for front-drive vehicles and is the reverse of the "rearward cross." On front-drive applications, the front tires move directly to the rear and the rears cross to the front opposites.

Figure C

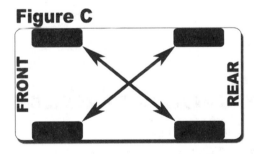

Figure C, the X-pattern, shows fronts changing with opposite rears and vice versa. This simple layout can be used in place of the rearward or forward cross; which pattern you choose should be determined after examining the tire wear patterns.

Figure D

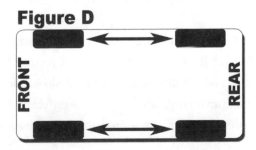

The directional (also called "uni-directional") tread design has proven popular as a way to build wet weather capability into performance tires, but it limits choices when rotating. Figure D shows the front-to-rear/rear-to-front rotation of same-size directional tires. Directional tires have indicators on the sidewall showing the tire shop which way they were designed to work. Never attempt to aim these tires in the opposite direction from the arrow as they were engineered to disperse water more quickly.

Figure E

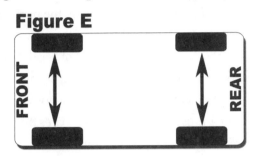

Some high-performance vehicles such as Porsches and Corvettes have different sizes of wheels and/or tires from front to rear, which means there is no conventional format for rotation. For those cars, it is recommended that tires be separated from the wheel, mounted on the opposite wheel, and rebalanced before installation. Figure E shows this same-axle rotation. Initially, it will cost a few dollars more to follow this practice, but in the long run the savings on prematurely worn tires will be worth it.

The mark on this ultra high-performance Nitto N404 SUV tire indicates the uni-directional tread can only be rotated from front to rear on the same side.

THE 26 CENT TIRE SAFETY KIT

There is a gauge whose sole purpose it is to measure the tread depth of passenger car tires, but when was the last time you had one in your pocket when you needed it?

Amazingly, former presidents Washington and Lincoln are always around to help motorists determine when tire tread is no longer safe. For 26 cents, the value of one U.S. quarter and penny, you have all the information you need about tread depth in one convenient kit.

The top of Abraham Lincoln's head on the penny is approximately 2/32-inch from the top of the coin. Insert the penny upside down between two blocks of tread; if you can see air above the 16th president's noggin, it is time to buy new tires. Most states will not pass a vehicle for inspection if the tread measures less than 2/32-inch. Tires this low on tread will exhibit great dry pavement handling, but will easily hydroplane in the wet and be completely useless in snow.

This Hoosier tire is not worn out—it's brand new! It is intended for competition, and its tread has been shaved to allow greater dry pavement traction. Your street tire, however, should never look like this. (Photo Tire Rack)

George Washington's white locks are 4/32-inch from the edge of a quarter. Coincidentally, this depth corresponds to a tread level considered the minimum for driving in wet, rainy conditions. As the tread blocks become smaller through wear, the channels they create between them to force water away from the footprint are minimized. Driving in the rain with 4/32-inch tread is just sufficient for light rain, although standing water is likely to cause a momentary loss of control at speed.

If your current tires are going to be called upon for snow duty, it is recommended they have a minimum tread depth of 6/32-inch—roughly the distance from the top or bottom of the Lincoln Memorial on the back of a penny to the edge of the coin. Deeper tread enhances the tire's ability to cut through snow and gain traction; anything less

Tread wear indicators (Photo Falken)

can cause the tire to spin without advancing the car.

Despite the ease of this time-honored coin trick, many people do not check their tires regularly for tread depth. Fortunately, they can rely on a built-in backup in the form of "wear bars" that become more visible as the tread reaches its minimum. Some tires designed for winter use are equipped with two levels of tread bars—the first indicating 6/32-inch has been reached and the second becoming visible at 2/32-inch.

Depending on their manufacturer and function, the tread on new tires measures in this range:

performance	**10/32-inch**
passenger	**10.5 to 11/32-inch**
truck/SUV	**12 to 16/32-inch**
all-terrain	**16 to 18/32-inch**
off-road	**15 to 20/32-inch**

FIXING A FLAT/BALANCING

When it comes to flat tires, there are punctures... and then there are PUNCTURES. Air loss from a tire can occur over a period of days through an opening the size of a pinprick or within seconds following removal of a penetrating nail or screw. Checking tire pressure once a week as recommended can prevent an interrupted trip if the first kind of puncture has occurred; it's time to get the spare tire out and do some roadside repairs if you encounter the second type.

No matter how quickly your tire is losing its vital compressed air, it is essential it be properly repaired immediately and not driven any further. A slow leak may not seem like an emergency, but as air of different temperatures meet at the damaged area, moisture forms and rusts the exposed steel cords, producing a situation that can severely affect a tire's integrity.

As a rule, most responsible mechanics will not put back into service any tire that has suffered a puncture greater than 1/4-inch in diameter or is located on the tire's shoulder or sidewall. Unless special conditions—such as being in the middle of the desert—warrant, no puncture should be repaired without first removing the tire from the rim for a complete visual inspection of the innerliner. Although the hole may look simple and clean from the outside, under the tread may reveal rusted ends of steel cord or a very large "exit wound" indicating the nail or screw swirled during driving and gouged more material.

Shops that insist on forcing plug material through the tread from the outside without removing the tire should be avoided. The most typical accepted means of puncture repair is a combination of the age-old flat patch with a rubber plug that is fed through the hole from the inside and cemented into place before the plug is trimmed flush from the tread side. It looks a bit like a capital letter T. Because the innerliner's rubber compounds are able to retain air and since the volume of gas inside the tire is always exerting pressure toward the outside, the combination patch/plug can be very effective in preventing further air loss if properly cemented to a clean surface. This cleaning involves the use of an abrasive drill-like awl that removes any rust or dirt.

Although millions of tires have been properly repaired and driven problem-free, be aware that manufacturers are reluctant to maintain a product's speed and load ratings after a puncture and that warranties may not be honored should the tire fail after such a repair. It is also not recommended that street or competition tires be used for track events after repair.

Dynamic balancing should follow any removal of the tire from the wheel. Again, this is a task that can only be performed by a skilled technician with proper tools and equipment.

To the dictionary, balance means a uniform distribution of mass about the wheel's axis of rotation (center). To the driver, balance means there is no side-to-side vibration through the car's steering wheel or other part of the chassis. Balancing wheels and tires is vital if a long tread life and even wear are to be had.

The worst kind of imbalance (on otherwise good components) is when the high (or heaviest) spot on a tire is closely aligned to the high spot on the wheel, effectively doubling the problem. In this scenario, a wheel and tire will literally throw themselves into the air and against the ground as centrifugal force swings the rolling stock like a sock full of quarters. A good technician will loosen the tire and rotate it 180 degrees and run it on the machine to see if the imbalance has subsided or gone away. If that doesn't do the trick, he might then rotate 90 degrees on a third attempt and another 180 degrees for a fourth try. Unless the wheel has been damaged or the tire is suffering from some internal malady, placing the tire against each of the wheel's four corners should solve the problem.

FIXING A FLAT/BALANCING

Our local Muffler Masters in Kannapolis, N.C., is a busy garage that repairs quite a few flats every week in addition to its exhaust, brake, alignment, and tow equipment business. Billy Owens took us step-by-step through the process of repairing a flat tire. We don't recommend anyone try to mount, balance or repair tires without the proper equipment and training. It can be a very dangerous job if not properly prepared and protected. (Photos Brad Bowling)

1. Owens takes the injured tire off of a customer's Honda Passport.

2. The first step is to remove the clip-on weights from the rim. This will prevent damage during the process of unmounting the tire. He also removes the valve mechanism from the stem to release air pressure.

3. From the rear of the wheel, Owens removes the screws that secure the center cap.

4. Separating the tire's bead from the wheel's bead seat is an easy task with this specialized machine. Here, the front side is separated.

5. Owens manually flips the wheel and separates the other side of the rim from its bead.

6. Owens moves the wheel to the horizontal mount where the bead will be slipped over the rim flange for removal.

7. The machine slips around the rim, lifting both beads over the edge of the tire.

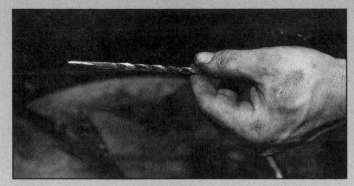

8. Owens reams the puncture opening with this sharp awl in order to clean it and strip away any rusted steel belt ends.

9. (Straight plug method) Taking a strip of plug material, Owens threads it through the end of this tool.

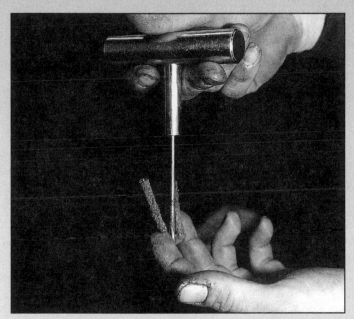

10. (Straight plug method) It's ready to be inserted through the tread from the outside.

11. (Combination plug/patch method) This is the plug/patch as it comes out of the box. The metal sheath allows the plug to be forced through the puncture from inside the tire.

12. (Combination plug/patch method) Here is what the actual plug/patch looks like.

13. Anything between Owens' fingers is safe for making a simple repair. This area lies between the shoulders of the tire.

14. With the hole repaired to his satisfaction, Owens applies a soapy solution to the bead of the tire in order to facilitate re-mounting it.

15. The same machine that slid the tire off of the wheel slips the beads over the rim flange for mounting.

16. Owens uses compressed air to force the beads against their seats. Once the two loud pops are heard, he uses the machine's built-in gauge to fill the tire to its proper pressure.

17. This tool installs a new valve mechanism in the new stem so the pressurized air doesn't rush back out.

18. Next comes the computer balancing machine.

19. The array of clip-on weights range from .25 ounces to 5.0 ounces each.

20. The weight with the shorter clip is for steel wheels; the longer clip is for alloys.

21. Owens installs the wheel and tire on the machine, where it will be spun to check for balance.

22. This board will tell its operator everything he needs to know about the balance of the mounted wheel, including where to place different weight amounts.

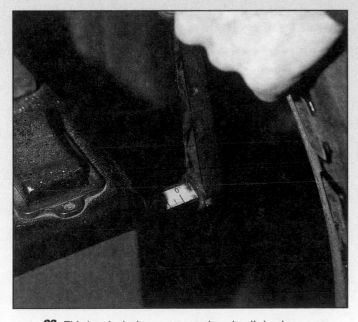

23. This handy device measures the wheel's backspace.

24. These calipers measure the wheel's true width.

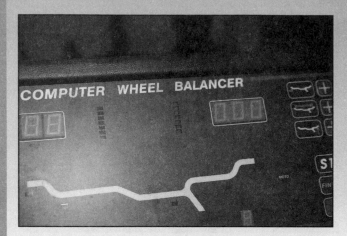

25. After the machine spins the tire to find its high spots, Owens can move it by hand and these lights indicate exactly where the weight or weights should be mounted.

26. This tire balanced well with just one small weight on the outside of the rim. After this, Owens puts the repaired and balanced tire back on the Honda.

NEW TIRE BREAK-IN

Although the days of extended break-in periods for new car engines are over, it is still recommended that tires be given special treatment during their first 500 miles of use. The primary reason for this recommendation is a lubricant that manufacturers use during the molding process to keep tires from sticking—just as butter works to keep your skillet and grilled cheese sandwich from becoming one. Until it wears off through cornering and braking, traction will be slightly affected.

Tires hot off the assembly line are as fresh as a new loaf of bread. A break-in period is recommended to allow them to perform at their best. (Photo Goodyear)

Because of the various components of rubber, steel, and fabric that make up the tire, a break-in period free of excessive heat and stress also ensures a smooth working relationship.

One last reason to follow the 500-mile break-in rule is that it will provide time to get accustomed to the "squirminess" of the new tires. People usually don't buy new tires until the tread on their current tires is quite low—a condition that makes for great steering response and handling on dry pavement. New tires, wearing full tread, just won't handle as crisply until broken in.

DOT TIRE REGISTRATION

The Tire Industry Safety Council recommends registering your purchase with the manufacturer by way of a registration form available from your dealer. The independent dealer is not responsible for contacting you in the event of a product recall, but the manufacturer and manufacturer-owned dealership are.

The owner of a recalled tire is entitled to a replacement, repair, or refund if it is returned within the time specified by the manufacturer.

For more information contact the Tire Safety Council, P.O. Box 3147, Medina, OH 44258.

During the infancy of the automobile, the term "tire technology" would have been an oxymoron had anyone thought to put those two words together. Those elongated rubber bladders people wrapped around wheels to smooth some of the road's vibration had only one thing in common with today's high-performance, high-mileage radials—they were round (most of them).

In the first two decades of the 20th century, automobile tires tended to fail, rupture, deflate, and disintegrate at a pace that would be unacceptable to modern drivers. Reliability was so poor that a smart automobilist kept several spares handy at all times. Although they were of pneumatic design, the hard rubber carcasses of early tires provided very little shock absorption. Because they were relatively skinny, traction over the mud- and snow-covered roads of the day was quite good, but cornering at speed was a feat undertaken only by fools and daredevils. In those days, all tires were created equal.

This modern reproduction of an early 1900s-era tire benefits from a century of technology. The real thing was not so lucky. (Photo Coker Tire)

Fast-forwarding to the '60s brings us to a time when a bias-ply tire could be designed for either comfort, longevity, performance, or rough conditions—but nobody had figured out yet how to combine any of these two or more traits. True, there were more choices for the consumer, but picking one type of tire generally meant forfeiting the other characteristics. Fortunately, improvements were on the horizon.

How would you like to a set of these on your modern SUV? Fortunately, advances in rubber, steel, and a lab full of chemicals have improved the product. (Photo Coker Tire)

Over the last two decades, great leaps have been made in tire technology, especially in the realm of the does-everything design. Sacrifice is no longer a requirement when shopping for new tires. It isn't necessary to give up wet traction for ultra-performance; off-road tires don't have to beat passengers silly when used on a highway; and a decent tread life no longer means buying rubber with the hardness of a cinder block.

Sure, compromises are still a part of the tire game. There's no design that's equally capable on a 200-mph Ferrari and a Baja dune buggy, for instance, nor is there likely to ever be one. The point is that manufacturing processes and materials are so advanced that a tire can rate excellent in one category and still be quite good in all others.

The following directory provides a sampling of the major tire brands and models sold in the United States.

BFGoodrich

PO Box 19001
Greenville, SC 29602-9001
www.bfgoodrichtires.com

- **compacts**

- **sports cars**

- **passenger cars**

- **trucks/SUVs**

- **off-road**

Just about everything in the BFGoodrich tire family revolves around the initials T/A. In the car line, T/As include the all-season Control, family car Touring, several high-performance street tires (the Comp, g-Force, and Scorcher) and many models for trucks and SUVs (Radial Long Trail, Rugged Trail, Open Trail, All-Terrain, Commercial, Mud Terrain, and Baja). Only the pedestrian Momenta and utilitarian Winter Slalom live outside the T/A family.

Scorcher T/A
(Photo Tire Rack)

g-force T/A KDW
(Photo BFGoodrich)

All Terrain T/A KO
(Photo BFGoodrich)

Krawler T/A
(Photo BFGoodrich)

Bridgestone

One Bridgestone Park
Nashville, TN 37214-0991
615-391-0088
www.bridgestonetire.com

- **compacts**

- **sports cars**

- **passenger cars**

- **trucks/SUVs**

- **off-road**

Shojiro Ishibashi founded the Bridgestone Tire Co. Ltd. in Kurume, Japan, in 1931. Because Ishibashi, whose surname means "stone bridge," was an admirer of Harvey Firestone's products, he paid tribute to the American firm by naming his in a similar fashion. Ishibashi was a producer of rubber-soled footwear when he became a tire manufacturer, and soon his quality products attracted the attention of General Motors, Ford, and Chrysler—all of whom were the leading automakers for the Japanese market at the time. Bridgestone began selling tires in the U.S. in 1967 and purchased Firestone in 1988. Today, the Bridgestone line includes more than a dozen different brands, starting at the top of the performance ladder with Potenza. In this case, "performance" is broadly defined as applying to everything from Taurus wagons to autocrossing Corvettes, with the RE730, S-02, and S-03 Pole Position models occupying the ultra-high end of the spectrum. Other lines that fall in the performance category are the Eager and Expedia. Touring tires, for the luxury car owners, can be found in the Turanza line, while the quiet ride/basic transportation market is well served by the Insignia SL, S402, and several others. Bridgestone's Blizzaks are legendary among drivers whose daily commutes might include several inches of new snow, ice, or slush, but for serious low-traction environments, the Duelers have the more aggressive tread patterns off-roaders favor.

Blizzak LM-22
(Photo Tire Rack)

BT-70
(Photo Tire Rack)

Dueler HP D680
(Photo Tire Rack)

Potenza S-03
(Photo Tire Rack)

Turanza LS
(Photo Tire Rack)

Turanza LS-T
(Photo Tire Rack)

Coker Tire

1317 Chestnut St.
Chattanooga, TN 37402
800-251-6336
www.cokertire.com

- **vintage cars**

- **vintage trucks**

- **vintage motorcycles**

The vintage tire reproduction industry continues to grow every year, with more brands and models from the past being re-popped annually. Coker Tire is the world's largest supplier of vintage rubber products and, without a doubt, one of the most influential companies in the old car hobby.

Harold Coker, a collector car enthusiast in the days when "old" only referred to vehicles built prior to World War II and new cars had tailfins, started the Coker Tire Co. in 1958. Later, he was able to indulge his vision of reproducing out-of-stock tires from original molds and in 1974 handed his son Joseph "Corky" Coker the reigns to the fledgling antique tire division. The vintage tire sales initially represented less than 5 percent of the company's total business and was located in a 500-square-foot space at the back of the family's Chattanooga, Tenn.-based BFGoodrich dealership.

Today, vintage tires account for 95% of the dealership's sales, with shipments to every state in the U.S. and more than 32 foreign countries, and occupies 95,000 square feet in six buildings. During his years building the business, Corky located and purchased original molds from tire makers, sometimes traveling as far away as South America, the Philippines, and Australia in the process. In some instances, his craftsmen were able to reproduce molds from drawings when it was clear the original equipment could not be found or used. Rather than risk the family's financial health by building a dedicated factory, Corky negotiated contract production in Pennsylvania and Ohio for domestic supply, with manufacturers in Taiwan, Chile, Vietnam, and India supplying export customers.

Through his efforts Coker Tire secured the worldwide licensing agreements and exclusive distributorships to vintage brands from BFGoodrich (such as the famous Silvertown), Firestone (Wide Oval, among others), Michelin, and U.S. Royal. There is also a Coker Classic brand of tires and a variety of others.

BFGoodrich Radial (Photo Coker)

Classic Whitewall
(Photo Coker)

Excelsior Clincher (Photo Coker)

Firestone 500
(Photo Coker)

Firestone 890 (Photo Coker)

Firestone (Photo Coker)

Continental

1800 Continental Blvd.
Charlotte, NC 28273
704-588-5895
www.contigentire.com

- **compacts**
- **sports cars**
- **passenger cars**
- **trucks/SUVs**
- **off-road**

Since its founding in Germany in October 1871, Continental has become the fourth-largest tire manufacturer in the world. It ranks first in Germany and second in Europe overall. Output includes tires for industrial applications as well as for passenger cars and light-duty trucks. Its five North American plants produce one-third of its total passenger and commercial tires. In 1987, Continental bought General Tire, which it owns to this day. The passenger tire line includes the performance-oriented ContiSportContact, ContiSportContact 2, ContiExtremeContact, and ContiTouringContact series. The TouringContact AS is aimed at the luxury car owner and cold, inclement weather is the reason for the ContiWinterContact TS790. The truck and SUV market is served by the ContiTrac SUV and ContiTrac TR.

SportContact CH90
(Photo Continental)

TouringContact AS
(Photo Continental)

TouringContact CT85
(Photo Continental)

ContiTrac AT
(Photo Continental)

ContiTrac AW (Photo Continental)

ContiTrac SUV
(Photo Continental)

4x4 Contact
(Photo Continental)

SportContact 2
(Photo Continental)

TourContact CV95 (Photo Continental)

Cooper

701 Lima Ave.
Findlay, OH 45840
419-423-1321
www.coopertire.com

- **compacts**
- **sports cars**
- **passenger cars**
- **trucks/SUVs**
- **off-road**

Cooper began making tires in 1914 and, in addition to its line of automobile, truck, and motorcycle tires, manufactures inner tubes, NVH (noise-vibration-harshness) control systems, automotive sealing, and fluid delivery systems. It started life as the M and M Manufacturing Co., then was known for a brief while as the Giant Tire and Rubber Co. in Akron before Ira J. Cooper renamed it after himself in 1920. The company currently has more than 55 manufacturing and technical facilities in 13 countries and employs more than 20,000 people worldwide. Cooper produces several brands of tires for automobiles and trucks/SUVs, including Avon, Mastercraft, Roadmaster, Starfire, and Dean. A line of racing tires is produced under the Avon label. The Cooper line includes the Cobra (performance), Trendsetter (economy), Lifeliner (OEM replacement), Discoverer (light truck and off-road), and Weather-Master (winter).

Cobra GT
(Photo Cooper)

Cobra GTH S
(Photo Cooper)

Cobra GTZ
(Photo Cooper)

Discoverer A/T
(Photo Cooper)

Discoverer H/T
(Photo Cooper)

AST II
(Photo Cooper)

Classic II
(Photo Cooper)

Discoverer LT
(Photo Cooper)

Dayton

One Bridgestone Park
Nashville, TN 37214-0991
615-391-0088
www.daytontire.com

- **compacts**
- **sports cars**
- **passenger cars**
- **trucks/SUVs**
- **off-road**

Dayton is perhaps best know for its popular Thorobred Steel passenger car tire. Now the price leader brand of the Bridgestone/Firestone family, Dayton offers a Daytona line of high-performance tires that incorporates UNI-T technology developed for its more expensive corporate siblings. They come in Z, H, S, and T speed ratings. The Daytona Premium GT, with an 80,000-mile treadwear rating, is the brand's sole luxury car offering. Quadra, Thorobred Steel, and Daytona Metric Radial are available for everyday passenger car duty. Timberline, Daytona Radial Stag, and Radial Highway Service cover the light-truck and SUV range.

Dunlop

1144 E. Market St.
Akron, OH 44316-0001
330-796-2121
www.dunloptire.com

- **compacts**
- **sports cars**
- **passenger cars**
- **trucks/SUVs**
- **off-road**

Who knows what direction tire technology might have gone had it not been for Scottish veterinarian John Boyd Dunlop's invention of the pneumatic tire in 1888? From that first air-filled rubber tube—created for his son's bicycle—

to its recent acquisition by Goodyear Tire and Rubber, the story of Dunlop Tire now spans three centuries. The company produces a line of tires for every size, purpose, and type of vehicle, including high-performance passenger cars (SP Sport and GT Qualifier, to name two), everyday passenger cars (Axiom, SP series), and light trucks/SUVs (Grandtrek, Rover, Mud Rover). Dunlop also makes tires for ATVs, motorcycles, go-karts, and medium-duty trucks. Its run-flat technology goes by the name Dunlop Self-Supporting Technology (DSST), which includes a wheel-mounted pressure sensor.

Grandtrek (Photo Tire Rack)

SP Sport 5000 (Photo Tire Rack)

SP Sport 9000 (Photo Tire Rack)

SP Sport A2 (Photo Tire Rack)

SP Winter Sport M2
(Photo Tire Rack)

Sport Rover GTX 2 (Photo Tire Rack)

10404 Sixth St.
Rancho Cucamonga, CA 91730
909-466-1116
www.falkentire.com

- **compacts**
- **sports cars**
- **passenger cars**
- **trucks/SUVs**
- **off-road**

The Falken Tire Corporation, established in 1991 (formerly Empco), is a subsidiary of The Ohtsu Tire and Rubber Co. of Osaka, Japan. Falken currently produces a line of tires for light trucks and SUVs and several series designed for passenger, high- and ultra-performance applications. Truck series include S/TZ-01, S/TZ-04, Landair HT, Landair AT, and Radial AP. Car tires include Azenis Sport, Azenis ST-115, FK-451, Ziex Ultra Low Profile, Ziex 60 & 65, Ziex 512, and Sincera SN-706.

Azenis Sport
(Photo Falken)

Azenis ST-115
(Photo Falken)

FK-451
(Photo Falken)

S/TZ-04
(Photo Falken)

Ziex 512
(Photo Falken)

One Bridgestone Park
Nashville, TN 37214-0991
615-391-0088
www.firestone.com

- **compacts**
- **sports cars**
- **passenger cars**
- **trucks/SUVs**
- **off-road**

Harvey S. Firestone founded The Firestone Tire & Rubber Co. in Akron, Ohio, in 1900 to make solid rubber tires for carriage wheels. Soon his company was producing automobile tires for Henry Ford's Model T. Motorsports success soon followed when Ray Harroun's Marmon Wasp won the inaugural Indianapolis 500 in 1911 on Firestone's tires. Seven decades later, Firestone's Firehawk earned its reputation for high-performance in the 1980s during the brand's title sponsorship of a Sports Car Club of America racing series. Today, Firestone uses the name across a range of applications, but it is still a Firehawk—the SZ50 EP—that occupies top position on the company's performance lineup. Built using Firestone's UNI-T AQ technology (a system that gives the tire greater consistency in its performance, even as it wears over time) and available with RFT (run flat technology), the SZ50 EP touts the company's long involvement with the Indianapolis Motor Speedway with the label, "Born at Indy, Performs Everywhere." Affinity is the touring tire, while a variety of alphanumeric models (such as the FR380 and F-570) handle everyday driving

Firehawk Indy 500
(Photo Tire Rack)

Firehawk SZ50 EP
(Photo Tire Rack)

demands. The Winterfire, Firehawk PVS, and Town & Country Super Radial take care of the white stuff. Light-duty truck and SUV tires include the Wilderness range, Steeltex, and Destination. There is also a Firehawk designed just for the rigors of police and emergency service—the V-rated PV41.

General Tire

1800 Continental Blvd.
Charlotte, NC 28273
800-743-7075
www.contigentire.com

- **compacts**

- **passenger cars**

- **trucks/SUVs**

- **off-road**

General offers a full range of tires for most modern applications, sizes and purposes. The XP2000, known as the company's high-performance model since the late '80s when Saleen Autosport and others campaigned in the Sports Car Club of America's Showroom Stock series, has evolved into an all-season, all-purpose performance tire. General's all-new Exclaim, featuring an asymmetric tread design, now heads the list of performance tires for cars. Touring tires include an XP2000 GT and the Ameri* series. General's light-duty truck and SUV tires run the range from all-season highway use to serious off-roading, with AmeriTrac, Grabber, and Ameri* handling the soft stuff and Grabber AT2 and MT2 taking on the extreme conditions.

Ameri G4S (Photo General)

Grabber AP
(Photo General)

Grabber AT (Photo General)

Grabber MT
(Photo General)

XP2000 H4 (Photo General)

XP2000 V4
(Photo General)

Ameri 550 AS (Photo General)

Ameri 550 TR (Photo General)

XP2000 Z4 (Photo General)

Goodyear

1144 E. Market St.
Akron, OH 44316-0001
330-796-2121
www.goodyear.com

- **compacts**

- **sports cars**

- **passenger cars**

- **trucks/SUVs**

- **off-road**

Like almost all of the tire companies listed in this book, Goodyear supplies much of its production to the auto manufacturers. Goodyear's list of clients includes Italian supercar builder Ferrari as well as every single team on the NASCAR Winston Cup circuit. When it comes to Goodyear, the name to know for performance is Eagle. With technology developed through decades of NASCAR and Formula 1 racing, the Eagle offers a range of high-tech safety and performance features, including improved wet handling and run-flat technology. For the luxury crowd looking to go fast, there are the Eagle LS and GA. The GT+4 is the all-season performer. For stock car fans, nothing could be more exciting than showing off a set of the company's Eagle #1 NASCAR tires at the next race. The go-fast fanatics will flock to the uni-directional F1, which wears a tread design so slick it looks like it's already in motion. Passenger tires include the all-purpose Invicta, Integrity, Club, Regatta 2, and Aquatred. Foul weather driving is handled by the Eagle M+S, Ultra Grip and Ultra Grip Ice. Wrangler is to Goodyear's truck and SUV market what Eagle is to its performance models—in a range of street or aggressive treads—not to mention the Fortera, Conquest, and Workhorse. Goodyear is one of the four major tire manufacturers developing and promoting the PAX "inner wheel" safety design that seeks to eliminate the need for spare tires in automobiles.

Integrity
(Photo Goodyear)

Fortera (Photo Goodyear)

Aquasteel EMT
(Photo Goodyear)

Eagle F1 for Ford GT
(Photo Goodyear)

NASCAR (Photo Goodyear)

PAX (Photo Goodyear)

Eagle F1 for truck
(Photo Goodyear)

Eagle LS
(Photo Goodyear)

Wrangler MTR (Photo Goodyear)

Hankook

1450 Valley Rd.
Wayne, NJ 07470
800-HANKOOK
www.hankooktireusa.com

- **compacts**
- **sports cars**
- **passenger cars**
- **trucks/SUVs**
- **off-road**

Hankook, based in Seoul, Korea, is one of the world's largest tire manufacturers and sells its products in more than 200 countries. Its performance reputation has benefited from the company's association with several racing organizations, including sponsorship of the Solo and Pro Solo divisions of Sports Car Club of America. Hankook's Ventus high-performance line includes a handful of uni-directional H-, S-, W-, Y-, and Z-rated tires and the all-season H101. Hankook takes the label "high-mileage" to a new extreme with its luxury-oriented H707 Mileage Plus GT, which is guaranteed for 100,000 miles of useable tread life. Buyers who aren't sure their current car will last that long can opt for the 85,000-mile 845 Mileage Plus model. Hankook offers the Radial H714 all-season touring tire in three- or four-groove tread construction. The W400 (available in three- or four-groove designs), Zovac HPW401, and Radial W404 handle foul weather driving. Like most tire companies, Hankook's offerings for light trucks and SUVs exceed that of its performance models, with the Dynamic series running the range from grocery-getting to Rubicon Trail duty.

Hoosier

65465 US 31
Lakeville, IN 46536
574-784-3152
www.hoosiertire.com

- **race cars**
- **hot rods**

Hoosier, a name familiar to any fan of racing in this country, began in 1957 when Indianans Bob and Joyce Newton began re-treading street tires with softer compounds for better grip. This "mom and pop" company took its name from Bob's association with the Midwestern short track circuit and its corporate color purple from his No. 4 race car. In 1962, Hoosier started production of its own race-only tire through an arrangement with the Mohawk Rubber Co. in Akron, Ohio. In 1979, the closing of Mohawk's Akron plant forced the Newtons to build the world's first factory devoted to the production of competition tires. National recognition came to Hoosier in 1988 when its tires won nine races during its debut on the NASCAR Winston Cup circuit. The following year saw the introduction of a street performance tire bearing the now-famous name. Hoosier Tire is today the world's largest producer of competition tires, with facilities that include a 300-mph test track and state-of-the-art distribution center. Its Plymouth, Ind., factory manufactures 1,000 different models, including a small line of street tires aimed at the hot rod and Pro Street crowd.

A3S03 (Photo Tire Rack)

Interco

PO Box 6
Rayne, LA 70578
337-334-3814
www.intercotire.com

- **trucks/SUVs**
- **off-road**
- **race cars**

The Interco Tire Corporation has evolved through three generations of Louisianans to represent a major segment of the specialized high-performance off-road and 4x4 tire market. Interco's mind-boggling array of truck tires includes virtually nothing for the leather-lined, television/ DVD-equipped SUV soccer mom crowd. You won't be putting anything Interco makes on your grocery-getter, unless you happen to be a prospector or scorpion hunter living in Moab, Utah, or Point Barrow, Alaska, and getting to your local food source requires knowing emergency survival skills. The company's TrXus Mud Terrain and TrXus STS come closest to fitting the needs of the daily driver, with more conventional truck tread designs but still capable in sand and snow. Interco's Super Swamper series includes the TSL (the most recent iteration of the original 78-series off-road Swamper tire), the bias-ply LTB, TSL/SX (whose heavily treaded sidewall design gives it an evil armadillo appearance), Radial (it's either a smooth hard-duty tire or a very aggressive light truck tire), and Radial/TSL—all of which are DOT-approved and street legal. The Super Swamper Bogger features tread blocks so aggressive they resemble relief map versions of the crags and canyons the tires will no doubt visit.

TrXus STS
(Photo Interco)

TSL Bogger
(Photo Interco)

Super Swamper LTB (Photo Interco)

Super Swamper
TSL/SX (Photo Interco)

TrXus Mud Terrain (Photo Interco)

Kelly

1144 E. Market St.
Akron, OH 44316-0001
330-796-2121
www.kelly-springfield.com

- **compacts**

- **sports cars**

- **passenger cars**

- **trucks/SUVs**

- **off-road**

Edwin S. Kelly founded the Rubber Tire Wheel Co. in Springfield, Ohio, in 1894, to produce tires for the carriage trade, and in the century hence the company has gone through many changes in name and management. In only four years, it sold 45,000 carriage tires. In its first century in business, it had sold more aftermarket tires than any other company in the world. Renamed Kelly-Springfield in 1914 and purchased by rival Goodyear in 1935, the company survived two world wars and the Great Depression. Today it exists alongside Dunlop under the Goodyear corporate umbrella and produces tires for an enormous range of applications, including agricultural, industrial, and recreational. Its Charger line of performance tires for cars includes the W-rated (to 168 mph), uni-directional ZR;

asymmetric, H-rated (to 130 mph) HR; and H-rated Ultra HR765. The top-line all-season passenger tire is the Navigator Platinum TE with an 80,000-mile treadwear warranty and mud & snow (M+S) rating, followed by the Navigator Gold, Celebrity, Explorer and Metric 600T. Snow tires include the Magna Grip, Snowtrakker, and Wintermark radials. The popular light-truck and SUV market is served by the Safari line, which includes the Signature, SUV, AWR, SJR, and DTR models.

Navigator Platinum TE
(Photo Kelly)

Armorsteel KHS
(Photo Kelly)

SUV Premium (Photo Kelly)

Armorsteel KLHS
(Photo Kelly)

Safari Signature
(Photo Kelly)

Kumho

14605 Miller Ave.
Fontana, CA 92336
800-HI-KUMHO
www.kumhotireusa.com

- **compacts**
- **sports cars**
- **passenger cars**
- **trucks/SUVs**
- **off-road**

Beginning as Samyang Tire in 1960, this Korean company's average output in its first year was 20 tires a day. Thanks to a healthy export business to other Asian countries and a diversified linc that grew to include snow tires and aviation products, Kumho now exceeds 100 million tires a year and ranks in the top 10 world market. Performance tires include five ECSTA models, with speed ratings covering H (to 130 mph) to Y (to 186 mph). Passenger tire choices are limited to the 732 Touring Plus, a T-rated (to 118 mph) model. All-season tires include several S- (to 112 mph) and T-rated radials in most sizes. For serious winter applications, the I'zen Stud can be driven with or without studs.

ECSTA 711
Photo Tire Rack)

ECSTA KH11
(Photo Tire Rack)

ECSTA MX
(Photo Tire Rack)

ECSTA STX
(Photo Tire Rack)

ECSTA Supra 712
(Photo Tire Rack)

ECSTA V700
(Photo Tire Rack)

Road Venture AT
(Photo Tire Rack)

Road Venture HT
(Photo Tire Rack)

701 Lima Ave.
Findlay, OH 45840
419-423-1321
www.coopertire.com

- **compacts**

- **sports cars**

- **passenger cars**

- **trucks/SUVs**

- **off-road**

The Mastercraft brand is produced by Cooper Tire, along with Avon, Roadmaster, Starfire, and Dean. Mastercraft tires run the range from ultra high-performance (Avenger ZHP) to long-lived touring (Touring LX and Sensys 01) to deep-treaded off-road (Courser OTD Radial and Courser MT). Also included in the line are Glacier-Grip XT studless snow tires and popular truck and SUV applications such as the Courser HTR and A/T.

Avenger GT
(Photo Cooper)

Avenger ZHP
(Photo Cooper)

Courser A/T
(Photo Cooper)

Courser C/T (Photo
Cooper)

Courser HTR
(Photo Cooper)

Glacier-Grip XT
(Photo Cooper)

Glacier-Grip
(Photo Cooper)

HPZ-760 (Photo
Cooper)

Sensys 01 (Photo
Cooper)

Michelin

PO Box 19001
Greenville, SC 29602-9001
800-847-3435
www.michelin.com

- **compacts**
- **sports cars**
- **passenger cars**
- **trucks/SUVs**
- **off-road**
- **Space Shuttles**

Maker of the only tire to regularly go into space (attached to the landing gear of the Space Shuttle), Michelin produces an astounding number of wheels and tires per day from its 80 manufacturing sites around the world. When French brothers Edouard and André Michelin went into business for themselves in 1889, Edouard's idea for a removable rubber tire for bicycles soon put the company on the road to enormous prosperity.

In no time, their tire line expanded to include motorcycles, cars, airplanes—anything that had a wheel. Today, Michelin produces more than 21,000 types of tires. Eleven Pilot models make up the Michelin high-performance inventory, such as the uni-directional Sport and Sport A/A, the asymmetric Sport Cup and Primacy, and the comfort-biased Alpin. Its "performance luxury line" includes eight models, such as the long-life Energy radials, the MX Zero Pressure run-flats, and a variety of Pilots. Many of the passenger and luxury car series offer 80,000-mile warranties, including the XOne, Harmony, Agility, and Destiny. Truck and SUV owners have two dozen models to choose from. Michelin is one of the four major tire manufacturers developing and promoting the PAX "inner wheel" safety design that seeks to eliminate the need for spare tires in automobiles.

Pilot Sport
(Photo Tire Rack)

Harmony
(Photo Tire Rack)

Cross Terrain SUV
(Photo Tire Rack)

Energy MXV4 Plus
(Photo Tire Rack)

LTX
(Photo Tire Rack)

Pilot Sport AS
(Photo Tire Rack)

Nitto

6261 Katella Ave.
Ste. 2C
Cypress, CA 90630
888-511-6761
www.nittotire.com

- **compacts**
- **sports cars**
- **passenger cars**
- **trucks/SUVs**
- **off-road**

Nitto refers to its offerings as the "Extreme Tire Line," a claim that lets you know right away the company's emphasis is on high-performance. The uni-directional 505 and 555 models are Z-rated (over 149 mph) and—like all of Nitto's line—feature a jointless bead wire; spiral wound, jointless cap and edge plies; high-density rubber bead filler; and a liner with a high halobutyl rubber content to prevent air seepage through the carcass. Nitto engineers claim these features reduce vibration, increase high-speed stability and enhance steering response in all the company's tires. Less "extreme," but still an aggressive design, is the uni-directional V-rated (to 149 mph) 450 for passenger car applications. The 450 is advertised as an "all-season ultra high performance radial;" its counterpart for trucks and

SUVs is the uni-directional V-rated 404, which carries an M+S specification for mud and snow. Touring models include the H-rated (to 130 mph) 460 and S- (to 112 mph) and H-rated 470. New to the Nitto line is the Terra Grappler all-terrain tire for light trucks and SUVs with off-roading intentions.

Pirelli

100 Pirelli Dr.
Rome, GA 30162-7000
800-PIRELLI
www.pirelli.com

- **compacts**
- **sports cars**
- **passenger cars**
- **trucks/SUVs**

Like several tire companies whose origins date to the turn of the 20th century, Pirelli & Co. was founded during the revolutionary "rubber boom." When Giovanni Battista Pirelli went into business for himself in 1872, the rubber passenger tire was still many years in the future—Pirelli was interested in producing general rubber goods. Soon, the innovator was riding the first wave of telecommunication by manufacturing insulated telegraph wires (1879) and submarine telegraph cables (1886). It wasn't until 1890 that the company took its first step toward becoming a legend of the automotive and motorsports worlds by producing its first tires for bicycles—passenger car tires would follow in 1901. Pirelli's Cinturato, the Italian company's first radial tire, was introduced in 1948—decades before that technology became widely available in the United States on passenger cars. Pirelli led the industry in development of low-profile tires in the 1980s, a segment of the market in which it still excels, due in part to its promotion of the "plus 1," "plus 2," and further concepts for aftermarket tire sizing. Along the way, Pirelli acquired tire producers Metzeler and Armstrong. Its name synonymous with ultra-high performance cars such as Ferrari and Porsche, Pirelli's flagship is the P Zero line, which includes the Direzionale, Rosso, Rosso Direzionale, Asimmetrico, and Nero. The

P/number series—P4000, P6000, P600, P7, and P700—are a good blend of high-performance and all-season capabilities. There is even a touring Pirelli called the Cinturato after the company's first radial tire introduced a half century earlier. Pirelli's offerings in the lucrative SUV market are the Scorpions—five different models that range in capability from high-performance to serious off-roading. Pirelli is one of the four major tire manufacturers developing and promoting the PAX "inner wheel" safety design that seeks to eliminate the need for spare tires in automobiles. It also offers its own line of run-flat tires called Eufori—a system that combines stiff sidewalls with a required air pressure monitor.

PZero Nero
(Photo Tire Rack)

PZero Rosso Asimmetrico
(Photo Tire Rack)

Scorpion Zero
(Photo Tire Rack)

Winter 210 Asimmetrico
(Photo Tire Rack)

Winter 210 SnowSport
(Photo Tire Rack)

Sumitomo

1120 Welsh Rd., Ste. 120
North Wales, PA 19454
800-895-1449
www.sumitomotire.com

- **compacts**
- **sports cars**
- **passenger cars**
- **trucks/SUVs**
- **off-road**

Although it is not a household name in the U.S., the Sumitomo company legacy extends into history more than 350 years. Masatomo Sumitomo opened a book and medicine shop in Kyoto, Japan, early in the 17th century that diversified into fields of copper mining, finance, insurance, steel, real estate, and trade. Today, Sumitomo is recognized as one of Japan's leading business groups and its self-named tires represent the premium export of subsidiary Sumitomo Rubber Industries. Founder Masatomo could not possibly have predicted the invention of the automobile for which his company would eventually supply products, but Sumitomo features a wide range of applications and capabilities. Performance tires, which run from aspect ratios of 35 to 70, include the uni-directional, Z-rated (over 149 mph) HTRZ II; all-season, Z-rated HTR+; H-rated (to 130 mph) and mud & snow (M+S) capable SR1XON4; uni-directional, W-rated (to 168 mph) HTRZ; and H-rated HTR4. Touring is made up of the mud & snow capable SC 990, HTR TourA, and Cyclone Radial GT, plus the 40,000-mile SC 628. SUV and light truck owners will find a lot of models to choose from in the Sumitomo line, including the HTR Sport A/T, Serengeti Touring A/S, Serengeti Radial A/T, Durango XTR, Durango M/T, and Sonoma—all rated for mud & snow. Sumitomo is one of the four major tire manufacturers developing and promoting the PAX "inner wheel" safety design that seeks to eliminate the need for spare tires in automobiles.

HTRZ
(Photo Tire Rack)

HTR 200
(Photo Tire Rack)

HTR Sport AT
(Photo Tire Rack)

HTRZ II
(Photo Tire Rack)

HTR+
(Photo Tire Rack)

SR1XON 4
(Photo Tire Rack)

Toyo

6415 Katella Ave.
2nd Floor
Cypress, CA 90630
800-678-3250
www.toyo.com

- **compacts**

- **sports cars**

- **passenger cars**

- **trucks/SUVs**

- **off-road**

Toyo tires have several innovations applicable to most of its range, such as a built-in rim flange protector (a slight protrusion from the sidewall that helps reduce damage to wheels from low-speed curb contact), high-elongation steel cord belts (borrowed from the off-road tire industry, but used in many of Toyo's street tires) and spiral winding of its outermost nylon cord to eliminate overlap joint splicing of the underlying steel belts. The top of Toyo's ultra-performace heap would have to be its uni-directional, Z-rated (over 149 mph) Proxes T1-S tire, which is also available in V (to 149 mph), W (to 168 mph), and Y (to 186 mph) speed ratings. Other Proxeses in the ultra category include the all-season FZ4 and Z1, DOT-approved competition RA-1 and SUV-sized S/T. Passenger car tires include the 65,000-mile Proxes TPT (in H or V speed rating), Spectrum, 800 Ultra, and the "severe snow"-rated Observe. Light truck and SUV models range from the civilized (Open Country A/T, Proxes S/T and M410) to the dirt-churners (Open Country M/T and M55).

Proxes TPT
(Photo Toyo)

Open Country AT
(Photo Toyo)

FZ4
(Photo Toyo)

800 Ultra
(Photo Toyo)

T1S
(Photo Toyo)

PO Box 19001
Greenville, SC 29692-9001
877-UNIROYAL
www.uniroyal.com

- **compacts**

- **passenger cars**

- **trucks/SUVs**

- **off-road**

Since its origin in 1892 as the U.S. Rubber Co., Uniroyal has secured its reputation as a maker of dependable and affordable tires. It currently offers four models with its patented NailGard—one of the simplest, yet most effective, of the flat-preventing technologies. NailGard is a sealant that coats the inner liner of the tire and can seal punctures up to 3/16-inch in diameter. Uniroyal's Tiger Paw series is specified for passenger car and minivan use, while the Laredo is suggested for pickup trucks and SUVs.

Tiger Paw Touring HR
(Photo Uniroyal)

Tiger Paw AWP
(Photo Uniroyal)

Laredo All-Season AWP
(Photo Uniroyal)

Tiger Paw NailGard
(Photo Tire Rack)

601 S. Acacia Ave.
Fullerton, CA 92831
800-423-4544
www.yokohamatire.com

- **compacts**

- **sports cars**

- **passenger cars**

- **trucks/SUVs**

- **off-road**

Although it's only been in the lucrative U.S. market since 1969, Yokohama is the seventh-largest producer of tires in the world. Yokohamas have been spec tires for several IMSA and CART racing series, so it is no surprise the name is often associated with high-performance. The Z-rated (over 149 mph) A032R is one of the most aggressively styled street tires available—it looks like purpose-built race rubber with some wide, V-shaped lines carved into the tread to get past the Department of Transportation. Other uni-directionals in the ultra-high performance Yokohama line include the AVS Sport, AVS ES100, and AVS dB (so named with the symbol for decibel because it is the company's quietest ultra-performer). The Z-rated (over 149 mph) Parada Spec-2 is an asymmetric design aimed at the hot tuner/import market, with diameters ranging from 16 to 19 inches. Avid is the name of the high-performance line, with models including the H4/V4, T4, and S/T. Standard passenger cars include the Avid Touring and Aegis LS4. The company's winter tires, the Guardex 721, Guardex 720, and Geolandar I/T+, are rated for "severe snow" and feature blocky tread patterns with plenty of grip. SUV and pickup truck owners can choose from a range of capable models, from the conservatively styled Avid S/T, AVS S/T, and Geolandar H/T-S, to the seriously foul driving conditions the Geolandar A/T+11 and Geolandar M/T were designed for.

Avid S/T
(Photo Tire Rack)

Geolandar H/T-S
(Photo Tire Rack)

AVS ES100
(Photo Tire Rack)

Geolandar M/T
(Photo Tire Rack)

AVS Sport
(Photo Tire Rack)

Geolandar T/T-S
(Photo Tire Rack)

Geolandar A/T Plus
(Photo Tire Rack)

Parada Spec-2
(Photo Tire Rack)

SECTION TWO
WHEELS

WHEEL HISTORY

At the turn of the 20th century, car enthusiasts—then known as "automobilists"—had limited choices for accessorizing as we now know it. Wheels were primitive combinations of wood and iron, with only the occasional pinstripe of color giving some life to the design. Ford's Model T, the all-black icon of an America on the move, sported wheels measuring 30 inches in diameter by 3 to 3.5 inches in width. This setup was pretty much standard for mass-produced cars of the time.

Wire spoke wheels, usually combined with softer, wider tires than before, made their debut on many cars as optional equipment in the mid-1920s. Their introduction helped further separate the automobile from the horse-drawn carriages of the last century, and they provided a slightly better ride. These stylish rims evolved through the 1930s, developing shorter, thicker wire spokes until the auto industry's move to the stamped steel wheel—which was introduced in the mid-'20s on high-end luxury cars such as Cadillac as the "disc"—in the latter part of the decade.

Style was not an overriding concern for car buyers in the early 1900s. This 30 x 3.5-inch wood-spoke wheel is typical of the period. (Photo Coker Tire)

And there the clock stopped, it seemed, for wheel technology. Sure, diameters and widths fluctuated over the years, but Detroit was in love with its cheap-to-produce, trouble-free steel wheels. Change the trim ring and hubcap—for decades literally a small cover for the hub and lugs—and you've got yourself a new model to advertise. In the late 1950s and early '60s, "styled" steel rims, where the face of the wheel bore a design instead of a full hubcap, gained popularity among buyers of high-end and sporty cars.

The detachable rim design was a major step forward for wheel engineering. It allowed spare tires to be more easily mounted. (Photo Coker Tire)

Today the steel wheel continues a slow but determined evolution, with designs that mimic trendy alloy open-spoke styles at a much lower cost and at a lower weight than traditional stamped steel. Automakers have been equipping cars and trucks with steel wheels bonded to decorative plastic cladding that resembles popular alloy designs for several years—sort of a hubcap glued directly onto the wheel face.

With very little variation, the steel wheel reigned unchecked for several decades. (Photo Coker Tire)

Although we relied on them to get around for the past 60 years or so, production of steel wheels for car manufacturers is on the decline (currently 50% of that market) and just a blip on the aftermarket radar screen. The reasons for this drop-off are many, including the tendency of steel to corrode over time and the heaviness of the product when compared to alloys.

Lightweight alloy wheels were originally built from magnesium, but aluminum soon found favor with manufacturers because it was stronger, less corrosive, and would not ignite like magnesium. The light weight, great strength, and ability to assume many complex shapes sparked a consumer demand that steadily grew among enthusiasts through the 1970s and '80s until it exploded in the '90s with the proliferation of 18-, 19-, and ultimately 24-inch wheels. Enthusiasts were drawn to the aluminum wheels' reduced unsprung weight, improved acceleration and braking, more rigid architecture, and increased brake cooling through heat-conducting alloys and built-in venting.

ALLOY WHEEL TYPES

There are several processes for producing alloy wheels. Manufacturers choose one method over another based on what they want the final product to accomplish. Do they want the wheel to be inexpensive? Unbelievably strong? Extremely light? Have cutting-edge styling?

Casting, the most prevalent form of alloy wheel production, occurs when molten aluminum is poured into a mold and allowed to harden into shape. This is also known as gravity casting, since the aluminum fills the mold purely through the force of its own weight. The result is an inexpensive wheel that can be styled in a variety of ways. Retailers like cast wheels because they can be produced

for only twice what a stamped steel rim and hubcap might cost, but the downside is that cast wheels are the heaviest and least strong of the alloys.

Low-pressure or squeeze casting takes place when positive pressure is applied to the molten aluminum as it works its way into the mold—and in the process eliminates air from the mixture, creating a less-porous medium. This is the least complex and most common form of alloy wheel production that meets OEM specifications, but it produces a stronger and slightly more expensive rim than gravity casting alone. The surface of a pressure-cast wheel lends itself to chrome-plating well.

This SVT Lightning factory rim is made of cast aluminum. (Photo Tire Rack)

Speed Star Racing (SSR) produces this semi-solid forged wheel. (Photo Tire Rack)

Spun-rim or rim-rolling technology starts with a form of squeeze casting, but spins the result, heats the outer portion and uses steel rollers to press the rim into its final shape and width. Strength is close to that of a more expensive forged wheel. Many factory high-performance applications are the result of spun-rim production.

Forged wheels are the gold standard of the aftermarket. A billet of solid aluminum is forced through forging dies at an extremely high pressure. The result is very strong, light, dense, and expensive. If a one-piece wheel with great strength and performance potential is your top priority and money is no object, you want forged wheels.

Three-piece and two-piece wheels are very expensive and usually created for unique applications such as motorsports competition. In producing a three-piece wheel, the two rim sections are spun from a disc of aluminum, then bolted to a center and sealed with some type of adhesive to prevent air leaks. Originally developed for racing in the 1970s, three-piece wheels are popular in the larger diameters and are very expensive. Two-piece wheels feature a rim and center bolted or welded together. Prices for the two-piece designs are less than for the three-piece offerings, unless the center and rim are forged.

All of EVO's wheels, like this Axis SL, are made of forged aluminum. (Photo Tire Rack)

This BBS RK II is an example of a two-piece alloy wheel. (Photo Tire Rack)

WHEEL FINISHES

Semi-solid forged wheels are produced by heating billet alloy to the melting point and then forcing it into a mold at great speed. This process can nearly match the strength of forged products, but at a lower cost and with less complex machinery and tooling.

A good design is a thing of beauty all its own, but the overlaying finish can turn an alloy wheel into a piece of art.

The least expensive finish is tried-and-true paint. Colors can run the entire spectrum, covering black, white and everything in between, although the most common wheel hue is silver. When applied through powdercoating and covered by a clear coat, paint makes a very durable outer skin to protect a wheel. It is difficult to chip, does not corrode and can be maintained with any non-abrasive

ADR calls the paint finish on its MSport "Hyper Black." (Photo ADR)

cleaner.

A wheel with a machined finish is pretty much naked—the way it came from the mold—although a clearcoat is usually applied to prevent discoloration with age. A popular option is to have wheels painted, then partially machined so color and raw alloy are in sharp contrast. If there is no clear protective finish, maintenance can be high on

This Privat Fünf is an example of a machined and painted finish. (Photo Private)

machined wheels.

If an aluminum wheel is buffed to a high gloss, it is considered polished. Some applications can be made as shiny as chrome, but for a much lower cost. Chrome stays shiny longer if properly maintained, but minor scratches or blemishes on a polished rim can be buffed out to look like new.

Chrome-plating is hard to beat for eye appeal and it remains a popular choice despite its high cost. Nickel and

This OZ three-piece Superleggera has a polished lip. (Photo Tire Rack)

chrome actually work in concert to produce the mirror-like reflection. The result of the multi-stage process is a high-luster finish that is very durable and requires no clearcoat protection. It can, however, be ruined by harsh chemicals some automatic car washes use, so check with an employee or manager before subjecting your new $2,000 mirror-finish wheels to such abuse.

Chrome picks up every little reflection, as seen with this Panther wheel. (Photo Brad Bowling)

Investigate the cleaning chemicals being used at your local car wash because harsh solvents can easily streak chrome or clearcoated wheels. (Photo Brad Bowling)

WEIGHT, WEIGHT—
DON'T TELL ME

Ironically, today's heavy 24-inch chrome alloy wheels are the result of technology developed by people seeking ways to reduce weight in rims designed for motorsports competition. As processes to manufacture alloy wheels improved, the end products became stronger and lighter, leading some to interpret this as a call for ever-larger diameters.

It's equivalent to buying fat-free food but eating 10 times as much. "If *some* lightweight aluminum is good, then too much should be great!" is the thinking behind the current trend.

This is not to say we don't enjoy the massive components people are stuffing under their vehicles these days, because nothing could be further from the truth. If your car, truck or SUV is used primarily as a show vehicle or your time in the driver's seat is limited to Friday and Saturday night cruising, then wheel weight won't cause any sleepless nights. If, however, you are shopping for new wheels for a daily driver that needs to retain its nimble handling and braking in traffic and remain fuel efficient, pay attention to this section.

The subject of wheel weight and how it can negatively affect a car's handling and performance is seldom considered as part of the buying decision. Metal—even lightweight aluminum alloy—weighs more than an equivalent amount of rubber. Any addition to the wheel's diameter or width—assuming you are not increasing the stock overall diameter—replaces lighter rubber with heavier metal.

If an SUV weighs 4,500 pounds and your decision to buy four 24-inchers adds another 150 pounds above the factory equipment, that's about the same effect as gaining an average-size passenger, right?

Wrong. The important difference is *where* the weight is located and *how* it moves in relation to the rest of the vehicle's mass. A passenger contributes to <u>sprung</u> weight, which includes everything supported by the suspension components. Installing heavier wheels adds to the vehicle's <u>unsprung</u> weight, which has a direct bearing on responsiveness, handling, and braking. The entire suspension system of your vehicle—including the shock

A WHEEL BARGAIN

During research for this book we visited a local collector car dealership in search of aftermarket wheels. We discovered the smartest way to buy wheels and tires is with a car or truck already attached to them. Let someone else spend the big bucks.

This giant SUV, a two-wheel driven 1999 Ford Expedition XLT with 71,000 miles, borrowed from the Ford SVT Lightning parts bin. The previous owner resisted the temptation to super-size the rolling stock, which netted a few pounds of lost unsprung weight for the big Ford. It's wearing 18-inch SVT alloy wheels wrapped in 295/45R18 Goodyear Eagle F1 tires. At $16,900, this deal is like getting a free set of upgraded wheels and tires. (Photo Brad Bowling)

absorbers, springs, geometry, and bushings—was designed by engineers around a specific unsprung weight, a weight that stylin' upgrades can sometimes double.

Two other factors come into play when heavier wheels are installed on a vehicle. Inertia is the tendency of objects to remain at rest until acted on by an outside force. Momentum is the tendency of that same object to remain in motion until its energy is spent or an outside force interferes. In short, the more mass your wheel carries, the harder it is to start it rolling and also to stop it because wheels and tires become large, exposed flywheels as they spin down the road.

Try this experiment (even if it's only in your head). Turn a bicycle upside down and hand crank the foot pedal to get the rear wheel spinning. It takes some effort to overcome inertia, doesn't it? Once the tire has built up momentum,

If there were a Weight Watchers chapter devoted to cars and trucks, this chrome 24-inch Foose Spank and similar gigantic models would be put on the same list as Big Macs, deep-dish pizzas, and other consumables that make us sluggish and slow. (Photo Brad Bowling)

apply friction by placing your hand against the tread to stop the spinning motion. You can see it takes effort to play with inertia and momentum on a wheel weighing less than a couple of pounds. Imagine if you could reproduce this experiment with a full-blown 24-inch aftermarket wheel/tire assembly weighing more than 80 pounds. Not only would you likely lose a finger, break a wrist, or get a severe friction burn (this is your warning not to try it at home), but there would be no observable slowing for your effort.

Increased rotational inertia creates a drag on your engine's power output, resulting in slower acceleration and reduced gas mileage. By increasing rotational momentum, your brakes have to work that much harder to effect deceleration, which translates to shorter life for pads and rotors and longer stopping distances. In general, a vehicle

with radically heavier aftermarket rolling stock will feel sluggish compared to the same car with a factory setup.

It's important to be aware of these sacrifices before you buy your next set of wheels and tires so the decision can be an intelligent one.

The good news is that, size for size, an aftermarket alloy wheel will nearly always weigh less than what came on the car from the factory. If improved handling, braking, and chassis response are what you crave, stay with the stock size, but install a set of forged aluminum wheels. Even upgrading an inch or two in diameter and a half-inch to an inch in width should result in an unsprung weight decrease.

For example, a 14-inch factory steel wheel from Honda weighs approximately 18 pounds and a 15-incher runs about 21 pounds. Poring over catalogs reveals 14-inch alloys in a range from 8.9 pounds for a cast racing wheel from Advan to 14.5 pounds for a more practical cast wheel from Panasport, representing a reduction of 3.5 to 9.1 pounds per wheel depending on model. As diameters increase, the weight differential between factory steel or low-quality alloy rims and higher-grade equipment from the aftermarket is more impressive.

For a more common example, let's say your car currently wears 15-inch stock steel wheels and your goals are: 1) a better appearance and 2) improved chassis response. Because the average passenger car steel rim weighs around 22 pounds, it is possible to upgrade to any number of alloy 17-inchers and still lose weight. For example, the pricey but beautiful 17x7-inch OZ Superleggera weighs in at a featherweight 15.4 pounds, which would net our hypothetical buyer 6.6 pounds per wheel or 26.4 for the set. Several 17x7 models from Tenzo-R weigh in at 20 pounds each.

The simplest way to make an informed buying decision where weight is concerned is to place one of your current wheel/tire combos on an accurate scale, then compare that amount to listings for top candidates.

WHEEL SIZING

Unlike what we saw in the chapter on tires, wheel sizing is a very straightforward and easy-to-grasp concept with little knowledge of the metric system required.

The two most important dimensions to a wheel are

diameter and width. Diameter is simply the height of the wheel from the ground to its uppermost point. A tire's width is determined by measuring from the outboard side to the inboard side. About 99 percent of all passenger car and light truck wheels on vehicles sold in the U.S. fall in the 14-to-24-inch range in diameter and 6-to-10-inch spectrum for width.

(Photo Brad Bowling)

(Photo Axis)

OFFSET

Offset is the distance from the mounting pad of the wheel to the centerline of the wheel, typically measured in millimeters. Because we usually can't see the amount of offset built into a wheel when it's on the car, the consumer generally misunderstands this factor.

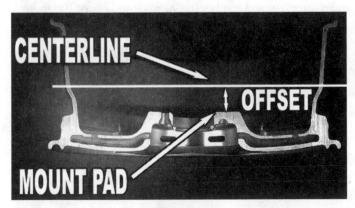

(Photo ALT)

In our example photo of a cutaway ALT alloy, the mounting pad is closer to the outboard (or street) side of the wheel. This is called *positive offset*, a situation most prevalent with front-drive and newer rear drive cars. Positive offset is growing in popularity as the design allows car manufacturers to cram more brake, suspension, and steering components into the wheel's interior and away from the valuable passenger, trunk, and engine

Positive offset
(Photo Brad
Bowling)

compartments.

In a case where the mount pad is flush with the centerline, a wheel is said to have *zero offset*. A "deep dish" design, where the mount pad is close to the inboard side of the wheel, is also known as negative offset.

Negative offset (Photo Volk)

Because the geometry of a suspension has been carefully engineered for optimum ride characteristics, changing the offset can negatively affect your vehicle's handling, tire wear, and even safety. It is possible to increase the width of a wheel, however, without altering offset by simply adding equal amounts to the inboard and outboard sides. A half-inch on the outside and a half-inch on the inside may not sound like much, but it produces a wheel that's an inch wider with no change in the offset. As with all upsize modifications, be aware that adequate clearance is essential.

No matter how much work you put into purchasing a new wheel, if the lug pattern and center bore were not designed for your application it will not work. Passenger cars and trucks today come equipped with 4-, 5-, 6-, 7-, and 8-lug rotors and drums. Each automaker seems to have a preference about which number to use for which vehicle class and whether to measure in metric or English.

A bolt pattern is measured as the diameter of an imaginary circle that crosses the center of each lug opening in the wheel. A 4-lug diameter might measure 100, 110, 130, or 140 millimeters in metric or 3.93 to 5.51 in English. A 5-lug system could run from 100 to 130 millimeters or 4.0 to 5.12 inches in diameter. The pattern is usually named by the number of lugs and its diameter. For example, 4 x 100, 4 x 4.50, and 5 x 4.75.

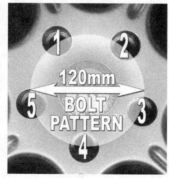

(Photo Brad Bowling)   (Photo Brad Bowling)

Some aftermarket wheels have as many as 10 lug holes drilled, the idea being that two or more lug patterns can be assigned to one center so the number of possible applications—and therefore sales—is increased.

More than one bolt pattern is built into this ALT wheel.
(Photo ALT)

With specialization in the wheel industry so rampant, it's no longer the case that one set of lug nuts can last a lifetime. There are three basic types of lug seats—conical/tapered, ball/radius, and flat—and a range of diameters and lengths to choose from. It is essential that bolts and openings are perfectly matched for shape and size.

Conical/tapered seat   Ball/radius seat
(Photo McGard)   (Photo McGard)

When installing or removing wheels, it is strongly recommended that a crisscross pattern be used on the lug nuts or bolts so as to relieve or increase pressure equally around the diameter of the pattern. Torquing the nuts or bolts should only be started with the tire high enough in the air that it is not in contact with the ground. A rule of thumb in the industry is that a bolt is properly tightened if it takes seven turns to torque it flush against the wheel, although some experts allow an extra half or whole thread.

A good shop will tell you to retorque lugs the first 25 miles after a wheel has been removed, and every 100 miles until the wrench indicates the torque is being maintained.

5-lug torquing pattern (Photo Brad Bowling)

The centerpiece of the bolt pattern on a hubcentric wheel is the center bore. This central opening is carefully sized to fit snug around the car's hub, which on modern cars is charged with supporting the weight of the vehicle with the lug nuts simply forcing the wheel's mount pad against the rotor or drum.

(Photo Brad Bowling)

The center bores of some wheels are purposely left slightly larger than the hub in order to allow fitment of a hub centric ring, which is simply an adapter that sits between the center bore and hub. Use of this ring allows a wheel to be installed when one lug pattern has several sizes of center bore.

Wheel spacers

In case you haven't seen a Pontiac television ad in the last few years, it bears repeating that a wider track on a car generally improves the vehicle's cornering ability. Not only do low-slung sports cars and sedans benefit from adding air between the left-and-right tires, but taller trucks and SUVs can reduce dangerous rollover tendencies by such a modification.

We promised in an earlier chapter not to subject you to a lot of high school math, so let's look at the wider track scenario in human terms. Stand with your feet together, directly beneath your body. If someone pushes you from the side, you will tip right over. Stand with your feet at shoulder width or more and the pushing force must be increased many times in order to get the same results. Because cars have relatively low centers of gravity and much greater weight compared to humans, a difference of 20, 40, or 60 millimeters (.8, 1.6 and 2.4 inches) is an improvement most drivers can feel.

LUG LOCKS

It is a good idea to have one locking lug nut on each of your wheels. Some automakers now install these clever safety features right at the factory on premium rims. One manufacturer of high-quality lug nuts—locking and otherwise—is McGard, a company whose color-coordinated and multi-faceted products have turned this lowly fastener into a fashion statement. For more information about McGard products, visit www.mcgard.com.

These 25mm DRA wheel spacers were designed for a BMW. (Photo H&R)

There are two relatively simple ways to widen the track of your vehicle should you decide to take advantage of this loophole of physical law.

The more expensive route is to buy a set of wheels and tires that are wider and/or have more negative offset based on criteria determined after performing careful measurements and calculations. Since you bought this book to learn about such equipment, no doubt you are already considering such a purchase, so this may be your chance to widen your vehicle's stance in addition to improving its overall appearance.

We can't supply all of the dimensions and other critical clearance information in this book for every car made, so tell a fitment expert what you want the new rolling stock to do, how you want it to perform, and what you want it to look like. A professional with hands-on experience can prevent a costly mistake.

A set of bolt-on wheel spacers—used in conjunction with your current wheels—would be a less expensive alternative. Just like the alloy rims they complement, spacers have come a long way in the last few decades. There was a time when spacers were made of questionable materials and applied to a wide variety of vehicles they may or may not have been engineered for.

Today, there are companies like H&R Special Springs selling such well-engineered spacers that they are used by several road racing series, including Porsches and Miatas. Manufactured in the land that gave us the Volkswagen and BMW, H&R's TRAK+ wheel spacers are constructed for specific applications from an aluminum-magnesium alloy that makes them 70% lighter than steel and just as strong—strong enough to be certified under ISO 9001 and German TUV standards. They are all hub-centric, so the weight of the car is not resting against the lug nuts and bolts—just like on modern vehicles.

Their product line covers the standard market range, with varying widths offered based on the vehicle owner's desired track increase.

- **DR model—10 to 40mm fits between the wheel and hub, with longer wheel bolts included in the package to make up the extra length.**

- **DRS model—10 to 40mm fits between the wheel and hub, exchanging existing wheel studs for longer ones; wheels are then fitted to the hub/spacer with existing wheel nuts.**

- **DRA model—40 to 60mm is fitted to the hub with special wheel bolts and has new threaded holes for existing wheel bolts.**

- **DRM model—40 to 90mm is fitted to the hub with special nuts and carries new wheel studs for the existing wheel nuts.**

The good news is that a set of spacers can widen the track of a car or truck for much less than the cost of new rolling stock. A scan over the H&R catalog shows spacers going for $70 to $200 for a set of two, depending on thickness and application—about 1/5th what you would spend for four mid-line alloy wheels and performance tires.

Wheel adapters

A similar product to the spacer is the wheel adapter, which is useful for mating wheels and hubs with different bolt patterns. Some people use the terms spacer and adapter interchangeably even if the spacer retains the same bolt pattern but has a different wheel mounted.

A true adapter is a go-between that mounts to the old pattern and provides a new one for the wheel. Because of the infinite combinations of cars and non-matching wheels, a good bit of homework is required to locate just the right piece of hardware. One of the more popular hot rod tricks in Germany is to fit Porsche factory wheels to everything from Audis to BMWs to Chevys and Fords—which explains the $190 H&R kit for that purpose.

The Tire Rack's headquarters is a shrine to round black objects.

Despite its name, the company offers a ton of alloy wheels as well.

This display in the office shows the difference 10 years made in the racing RX-7 wheel and tire.

A few laps around a tight road course in the passenger seat of a high-performance sedan would make a great lesson for elementary school children on the magical force of gravity.

Imagine a science classroom like that: The double overhead cam engine revs and the car flies forward. Rear tires chirp then grab. "Kids, notice how we get thrown back against the seat when I put 215 horsepower to the ground all at once? It's called acceleration, but it's what happens when Mr. Gravity wants us to stay in our seats."

The car approaches the skidpad at about 20 miles an hour faster than what sanity suggests and all four tires bite hard as the stiffly sprung car settles into the curve like it's got its own small-scale rail system. "See how the car tries to shoot off in a direction away from the center of this circle? Notice how your right cheek is now plastered against the window? Can you say 'lateral acceleration?' How about 'centrifugal force?' The car's not doing that—it's Mr. Gravity!"

After a few circuits of the skidpad, the car flies down a straight stretch of pavement and the teacher puts the four-wheel disc anti-lock brakes to use like a deer has just jumped in his path. "See why you always need to wear a seatbelt? You never know when a car might decelerate and Mr. Gravity will try to push your face into the dashboard or windshield."

Such is the dialogue I was having with my inner child as John Rastetter, the director of tire information services for The Tire Rack, piloted a blue Lexus IS 300 sedan through his company's onsite test track with me the wide-eyed passenger. Rastetter drove the little sports sedan like he had just stolen it and we were going to be the featured footage on *America's Scariest Police Chases*. Meanwhile, Mr. Gravity was having fun with my stomach.

It didn't seem like a very long track, but Rastetter used every inch of it. "The outer loop of the track is 1/3-mile long," he instructed. "The figure 8, which includes the skidpad, is also 1/3 of a mile."

I had ridden in and driven cars with equal

SLALOM

Sitting on 10 acres next to The Tire Rack's headquarters in South Bend, Ind., is a multi-purpose test track.

Sprinklers can provide wet weather at any time.

performance before—mostly race-prepped coupes or sedans with trick alignment settings, tires shaved nearly bald and suspension parts seemingly built out of solid rock. Those cars, with their exterior trim and carpet removed and utter lack of creature comforts, offered incredible handling and acceleration, but would have been torture chambers on the open road.

What was astounding about my time in the Lexus was its civility off the track, like when John drove it up the Interstate for gas and a wash.

The Tire Rack Lexus IS 300s were equipped with Eibach Pro-Kit springs and Koni Sport shock absorbers to give them a more stable platform than the stock car. Other than some stiffness over expansion joints and the sound of small gravel being thrown by the sticky Goodyear Eagle F1 GS-D3 high-performance radials, we experienced little sacrifice in the name of fast lap times. This Lexus was a great everyday car with a world-class sound system (which we didn't listen to), air conditioning (which we didn't need—Indiana was already air conditioned in December) and seats as comfortable as a La-Z-Boy recliner. It even had an automatic transmission, like all The Tire Rack test vehicles.

This skid of steel wheels will be mated with sets of winter tires.

What I got to experience was just another day on the job for The Tire Rack Team. From its inception in 1979 in Indianapolis to its virtual storefront opening on the Internet in 1996 to today's headquarters—a giant shrine to round objects located in South Bend—The Tire Rack is entirely focused on getting wheels and tires to customers.

The company's philosophy stresses its sales representatives be intimately familiar with its products. That intimacy starts with 8 weeks of intense classroom

The Tire Rack's stable of test vehicles includes this blue Lexus IS300.

instruction before fielding the first customer question as well as 80 hours a year of classes that include time on the track and 4.5-mile Real World Road Ride driving test vehicles.

The words "survey" and "feedback" get used a lot around The Tire Rack office and on its Web site. Online shoppers can find not only technical information about wheel and tire fitment, but how previous customers rated that particular product and what comments they wanted to pass along. Those online questionnaires go back to 1996 and recently included buyer feedback on as many as 618 different tire models in 51,795 individual surveys. Miles driven on the reported tires amount to a staggering 941,715,935—a few more trips to the mall and the billion mark is theirs!

"The reason the Web is so helpful for our customers," Rastetter speculated, "is because we already had the infrastructure in place to make it work. We had the customer service philosophy and the inventory to back it up. We didn't try to become an Internet company, just a tire retailer that sells on the Internet."

Another benefit of the database-driven www.tirerack.com is a guide where customers can locate a shop to install the products after purchase. These shops are usually nominated by Tire Rack customers, followed by The Tire Rack staff verifying they have the proper installation equipment (listing

costs for mounting, balancing, valve stems, and disposal) and customers comment on the service after the fact.

The Web site, produced in-house, also includes a virtual garage section where just about any combination of vehicle and wheel can come together in an instant for the buyer's consideration. Creating the hundreds of images of inventory is a full-time photographer whose studio on the first floor is large enough to photograph full-size SUVs. Print and electronic media are also produced in-house.

The warehouse is a model of efficiency, where an order taken in the afternoon can be on one of the

This display of wheels represents product being considered for sale by The Tire Rack. It is located where all sales personnel can appraise the products.

several waiting UPS and FedEx trucks that night. The tires are treated like ripe cantaloupe at the market, with great care and a lot of padding to prevent any scuffing or pressure. Seemingly endless lines of wheels and tires meet at the mounting and balancing equipment, where they are mated, aired up (in special safety cages), balanced, road force approved, and wrapped for shipping. A massive conveyor belt system runs like a scale-model Interstate throughout part of the warehouse, with its onramps and exits routinely routing wheel and tire families to different places and new adventures, one supposes.

Another section of the warehouse handles motorsports orders, with tires treated to heat cycling and run on rollers that break in the rubber for more durability. The Tire Rack is a familiar name to racers, especially in the American Speed Association (ASA), Sports Car Club of America (SCCA), BMW Car Club of America, and Brock Yates' One Lap of America series—all sanctioning bodies or clubs that benefit from the company's sponsorship and involvement.

During my visit, winter tire packages were popular items and I saw skids of plain new black steel wheels set aside for that purpose.

In addition to its wheel and tire lines, The Tire Rack has gradually been answering a customer demand for upgraded brake, suspension, and lighting systems.

"We've always considered the wheel and tire to be a combination product," Rastetter said. "By adding brakes and suspension kits, we are focusing on helping our customers enhance each corner of their vehicles."

The most innovative part of the company's

The walls of the company lunchroom are plastered with car movie posters.

philosophy is its insistence on testing products in order to give customers authentic appraisals of their value. The results of these tests, which are performed by many of the sales and management staff, are posted on the Web site. Evaluations performed shortly before my visit included "Taking Performance Tires to the Max," "Studless Winter Tires for Pickups, SUVs and Vans" and "Testing Bridgestone's 2nd Generation Potenza RE730."

Tests usually take place over a four-day period— Tuesday through Friday—and includes specific trips through the 4.5-mile public road test loop and the high-speed track at the facility. Since testers run the gamut from SCCA racers to everyday drivers, the results come from a good cross-section of personalities and skill levels. Because South Bend is smack in the middle of the snow belt, The Tire Rack crew gets plenty of opportunity to test winter tires; a local ice rink replicates the low-traction environment of a slippery street intersection when needed. Sprinklers on the test track can turn even the driest summer day into a downpour.

The tires being tested are not prepared in any special way for the evaluations; they are exactly as delivered to the customer and set to the air pressure recommended by the car's manufacturer.

The stable of company-owned test vehicles includes 3 Lexus IS300s and 3 Jeep Grand Cherokees. A Dodge Viper, 5-series BMW, Volkswagen Jetta and several other fun machines are owned by employees and function as long-term "real life" vehicles for tire evaluation. The blue Lexus I rode in had 17,000 miles on it. "It's about time to trade the Lexuses in," Rastetter told me. "We are getting a four-car set of matched BMW 330Ci coupes next. We like staying with rear-wheel drive cars because they provide more realistic information to the driver about what the tires and chassis are doing."

For more information about The Tire Rack, visit www.tirerack.com. Tell 'em Mr. Gravity sent you.

Custom rods, like this 1955 Thunderbird owned by Keith and Patsy Dorton, can look great with the right set of modern rims and high-performance tires. The Dortons chose 16-inch Center Line alloys and BFGoodrich radials all around. (Photo Brad Bowling)

Because new car manufacturers have provided more and more exciting models and styles to choose from over the last decade, the aftermarket wheel industry has enjoyed tremendous expansion and prosperity. The import crowd now has hundreds of lightweight alloy rims to choose from for its Acura Integras, Honda Civics, Mazda RX-7s, Nissan 240-SXs, Mitsubishi Eclipses, Subaru WRXs, and Toyota Celicas. Luxury SUV owners have dozens of triple chrome-plated 22- and 24-inch rims for their Lincoln Navigators, Cadillac Escalades, Ford Expeditions, Toyota Land Cruisers, Mitsubishi Monteros, BMW X5s, and Lexus GXs.

Alan Goodman's unrestored, all-original 1971 Ford Mustang Boss 351 still sports the optional Magnum 500 styled steel wheels from the factory and reproductions of the Goodyear Polyglas "low-profile" rubber. Several companies, including Wheel Vintiques, produce accurate reproductions of those vintage rims. (Photo Brad Bowling)

Audi TT with Borbet TD wheels. (Photo Borbet)

Finding just the right 17-to-18-inch rims for the traditional performance car—Chevrolet's Corvette and Camaro, Ford's Mustang, and Pontiac's Firebird—is now a matter of scanning the Internet for the perfect design.

Those of us who cling to the past have been rewarded for our loyalty with the return of many classic designs. With "retro" styling the rage among the world's carmakers, (who doesn't smile at the nostalgic styling of Chrysler's PT Cruiser, BMW's Mini Cooper, Volkswagen's New Beetle, or Ford Thunderbird?) wheel manufacturers have seen an increase in interest for old-timers such as Cragar S/Ss, American Racing Torq-Thrusts, and Center Lines of all types.

The following list of wheel companies, brands and models is not all-inclusive by any means. It represents more than 140 individual wheel lines available to the consumer, with contact information and an indication of what market the company serves. In some cases—especially where limited production foreign models are concerned—the contact information is likely to be that brand's distributor in the United States (such as Italy's Speedline Corse, which is imported by The Tire Rack in Ohio or Japan's Löwenhart, which is handled by Dazz Motorsport in California).

Please note that inclusion in this directory should not be taken as an endorsement for any company or brand. As with any large purchase, do your own homework before handing over money or a credit card number. Although many respectable citizens populate the aftermarket wheel industry, any field attracts the occasional fly-by-night operation. Deal only with reputable firms and those with good word-of-mouth endorsement among friends.

That said, here then is our directory of wheel brands—from AC Schnitzer to Zenetti.

AC Schnitzer automobile Technik
Neuenhofstr. 160
52078 Aachen
02 41/5 68 81 30
www.acschnitzer.com

- **BMW cars**

- **BMW SUVs**

In the mid-'80s Willi Kohl, one of the largest BMW dealers, and Herbert Schnitzer started AC Schnitzer and began producing a complete range of special accessories for all BMW models, including engine, body and suspension upgrades. AC Schnitzer's wheel line consists of three basic designs—Type I, Type II, and Type III—all available in single- or multi-piece construction. The five-spoke, star-pattern wheels range in size from 17 to 19 inches and fit all late-model BMW car and SUV models. There is even a series of wheels to fit the stylish new BMW-produced Mini Cooper.

Golden Apple Corp.
3532 Arden Road
Hayward, CA 94545
510-780-9800
www.adrwheels.com

- **compacts**

- **trucks/SUVs**

- **off-road**

Golden Apple Corp. has been supplying trim, spoilers, and other automotive aftermarket accessories to enthusiasts for more than 15 years. Four years ago the company entered into the custom wheel industry with its ADR Design for imported and domestic vehicles. ADR wheel models include the Tension, Exxes, Battle Exe, Domain, DSL, and DTM and range in diameter from 15 to 22 inches.

Type II
(Photo AC Schnitzer)

Type II
(Photo AC Schnitzer)

Type III
(Photo AC Schnitzer)

MSport Hyper Black
(Photo ADR)

Magnus Chrome
(Photo ADR)

Cypher Hyper Silver
(Photo ADR)

Aero

Wheel Country
888-810-6247

- **compacts**

- **cars**

- **trucks/SUVs**

Aero offers a line of alloy wheels measuring 15 to 22 inches in diameter. Available finishes for the Zeta, Fuego, Sujay, LaBanda, Dagga, Filero, and Tormenta among others, include silver painted, chrome, or polish.

Transa
(Photo Brad Bowling)

Fuga
(Photo Brad Bowling)

AFX Wheels

2301 Via Burton
Anaheim, CA 92806
(800) 813-1210
www.afxwheels.com

- **cars**

- **trucks/SUVs**

Wheel Effects originated in 1989 as an accessory supplier to the automotive industry, and in 1994 created its own wheel line named AFX. Wheel Effects is one of the few wheel companies to have its complete line manufactured and finished in the United States. Its truck line, which includes the Incline, Cliffhanger, Avalanche, Bandit, and Moab, runs from 16 to 23 inches in diameter. Sonix and Wedge, the two current wheel models offered for cars, run 16 to 20 inches. All wheels are finished in triple-chrome plating.

Akuza

Prestige Autotech
3366 Pomona Blvd.
Pomona, CA 91768
800-613-8889
www.akuzawheel.com

- **compacts**

- **trucks/SUVs**

Sizes range from 17 to 19 inches in diameter for car wheels and 18 to 22 for truck models. True to its advertising slogan—"Got Lip?"—Akuza designs wheels with some of the deepest lips available. Conscious of its popularity with the show crowd, Akuza boasts it has "a wet look silver finish that makes a statement of its own." With names like Fervor, Velocity, Rapacious, and Zone, Akuza speaks the language of its young, stylish clientele.

Alba

12850 Moore St.
Cerritos, CA 90703
877-921-0113
www.albawheels.com

- **compacts**

- **cars**

- **trucks/SUVs**

Bank, Twiz, Force, and Chromin are just some of the 15-to-22 inch triple-chrome wheels offered by this West Coast company. Alba manufactures and chromes all its own products.

Helix (Photo Brad Bowling)

Impulse (Photo Brad Bowling)

Alessio Alloy Wheels

9749 Crescent Center Dr. #201
Rancho Cucamonga, CA 91730
909-989-1103
www.alessiousa.com

- **compacts**

- **cars**

Wheel sizes run 13 to 18 inches for this Italian-based company formed by Andrea and Celeste Alessio in 1992. Alaska, Tour, Rally, Daytona, and Carerra are some of the models Alessio offers.

Polar (Photo Alessio)

ALT

11805 E. Smith Ave.
Santa Fe Springs, CA 90670
562-942-9597
www.altwheels.com

- **compacts**

- **cars**

- **trucks/SUVs**

ALT produces a line of beautiful 15-to-20-inch alloy wheels for many vehicles and lug patterns. Models include the traditional five-spoke Sonix, the ultra-thin spoke Vektor and Trax, the elegant Rival, the simulated three-piece Torq and the race-inspired LiteSpeed. Finishes include silver, chrome, titanium silver, bronze, or black.

210 LiteSpeed Silver (Photo ALT)

213 G-force Titanium Silver
(Photo ALT)

216 Vektor Silver (Photo ALT)

252 Rival Silver (Photo ALT)

254 Torq Titanium Silver (Photo ALT)

255 Meka Titanium Silver
(Photo ALT)

263 Kappa Bronze (Photo ALT)

267 Sonix Silver (Photo ALT)

269 Trax Silver (Photo ALT)

Alutec

The Wheel Exchange
555 Dynamic Dr.
Garner, NC 27529
888-682-3129
www.thewheelexchange.com

- **compacts**

- **cars**

Founded in 1996, this German company produces a variety of multi-piece wheels in the 13-to-18-inch range. The Zero, Kyro, and Evo Pro feature super-thin spokes, while the Leon, Java, VANtastic, and GT Pro are sturdy five- and six-spoke designs. All wheels are available in silver, with some models offering polished lips.

American Billet

shop.sportruck.com

- **trucks/SUVs**

Each American Billet wheels starts with 6016 T-6 aluminum stock. A custom center is machine-carved and welded to a spun aluminum rim, then polished to a mirror finish. These American-designed and -built wheels are available in a standard layout or with optional reverse-rim style, which gives the outside lip a smoother profile. Sizes range from 17 to 22 inches in diameter.

American Racing

1275 Davis Rd., Ste. 300
Elgin, IL 60123
www.americanracing.com

- **compacts**

- **cars**

- **vintage**

- **trucks/SUVs**

As one of the largest producers of aftermarket wheels, it is perhaps easier to ask what American Racing doesn't offer. From its roots in motorsports in 1956 through its acquisition by Noranda, Inc., an international natural resources company, American Racing has earned 18 patents and created more than 40 original designs, including its famous Torq-Thrust "D" model (which has made quite a comeback during the recent retro craze). It is also an original equipment manufacturer for Chrysler, General Motors, and Ford. AR's current catalog shows sizes ranging from 14 to 20 inches.

Teron (Photo Brad Bowling)

310 (Photo Brad Bowling)

39 (Photo Brad Bowling)

Torq-Thrust ST
(Photo Brad Bowling)

Torq-Thrust for truck
(Photo Brad Bowling)

Torq-Thrust D (Photo Brad Bowling)

The Tire Rack
7101 Vorden Parkway
South Bend, IN 46628
888-541-1777
www.tirerack.com

- **Mercedes-Benz**

Anyone with aspirations to one day own one of Germany's finest automobiles has heard of AMG. The company made its mark as a small tuner of Mercedes-Benz's sporty models and eventually was brought in-house to create a line of special high-performance models. Today AMG tweaks and modifies eight different M-B models, including the marque's two SUVs—all of which are sold through authorized dealerships with full factory warranties. Modifications and upgrades are made to the engine, suspension, brakes, and body work. AMG's line of alloy wheels is extensive, providing something for every current Mercedes model.

5-Spoke 211
(Photo Tire Rack)

5-Spoke 220
(Photo Tire Rack)

Double Spoke
(Photo Tire Rack)

Via G. Di Vittorio, 4
24030 Presezzo (BG)
(+39) 035697697
www.antera.com
www.eautoworks.com

- **cars**

- **trucks/SUVs**

Antera recently celebrated 10 years in the alloy wheel aftermarket business. Its eight wheel designs—mostly of the five- and six-spoke style—run from 17 to 20 inches in diameter for cars and 17 to 23 inches for SUVs. Model names, obviously picked by the engineering staff, include Type 329, Type 323, Type 321, etc.

Arelli

164 W. Jefferson Blvd.
Los Angeles, CA 90007
213-763-0930
www.arelli.com

- **compacts**

- **cars**

- **trucks/SUVs**

Assassyn, Bling-Bling, Skroll, Myth, and Kaz'Mir are just a few of the very ornate one-piece chromed wheels available from this West Coast company. Jade, Tempyst, Stylist, and Vetta are three-piece wheels produced by Arelli. The company offers a variety of lug patterns for sizes ranging from 16 to 22 inches.

Arospeed

10776 SW 190 Street #B
Miami, Florida 33157
866-276-7733, www.arospeedwheels.com

- **compacts**

- **cars**

Arospeed's RSGT, Riot, RS23, Crush, Static, Zoom, and Chaos alloy wheels are available in a variety of finishes, including silver, gunmetal, gold, white, and a "hyperblack." Sizes run 16 to 19 inches.

ASA

The Tire Rack
7101 Vorden Parkway
South Bend, IN 46628
888-541-1777
www.asaalloywheel.com
www.tirerack.com

- **compacts**

- **cars**

- **trucks/SUVs**

ASA was formed as a subsidiary of the Hankook Tire Co. in 1990 through an agreement with BBS in Germany—a relationship it continues to this day. In March 1992, the company began production of alloy wheels at its newly built plant and in October 1994, it received ISO 9001 status. ASA reached QS 9000 status—the highest quality management standard in the automobile industry originated by American big 3 car manufacturers—in 1999. The company is an original equipment manufacturer for Renault, Nissan, Daihatsu, Hyundai, Daewoo, and Kia and has an annual production capacity of 1.4 million units. ASA's current line of aftermarket wheels, from the impossibly thin Concept LS5 to the more conventionally sturdy Concept DD1, range in diameter from 15 to 18 inches.

FR1 (Photo Tire Rack)

LW5 (Photo Tire Rack)

TRS 2 (Photo Tire Rack)

ATA Touring Alloys

12850 Moore St.
Cerritos, CA 90703
877-921-0113
www.atawheels.com

- **compacts**

- **cars**

All ATA Touring Alloys have been custom crafted to fit the industry's leading European luxury/sport cars, including Audi, BMW, Mercedes-Benz, and Volkswagen. Additional fitments include: Acura, Honda, Infiniti, Lexus, Nissan, and Toyota. Its line of H10 through H60 wheels comes in 16- through 20-inch diameters and is available in silver or triple chrome finishes.

Atech

800-232-0734
www.hubcap-tire-wheel.com

- **compacts**

- **cars**

- **trucks/SUVs**

Running 16 to 22 inches in diameter, Atech alloy wheels feature a lot of variations on the basic five- and six-spoke design. Its 784, 785, 786, 787, etc. lines are available in chrome or silver finish.

629 (Photo Brad Bowling)

AT Italia

The Tire Rack
7101 Vorden Parkway
South Bend, IN 46628
888-541-1777
www.tirerack.com

- **compacts**

- **cars**

- **trucks/SUVs**

In 1992, after more than 30 years casting alloy wheels for the original equipment market, Paolo Tanghetti founded AT Italia in Brescia, Italy. Since then it has established itself as a company that blends engineering excellence with innovative and passionate design to create wheels that leave a lasting impression of quality and style. Its ISO 9001-certified labs have designed and use special equipment for the casting and production of alloy wheels, such as a procedure to apply a skin of polished stainless steel over the lip or the face of a wheel. The stainless steel lip is secured to the wheel in a patented process that is completed by a piece of equipment both designed and developed by AT Italia. This type of innovative engineering in wheel manufacturing as well as wheel design is of great importance in the overall AT Italia philosophy. Wheels range in diameter from 15 to 22 inches.

Inox (Photo Tire Rack)

Luna (Photo Tire Rack)

Type 5 Sport
(Photo Tire Rack)

ATS Leichtmetallräder

586-491-8383
www.ultimatefinish.com

- **compacts**

- **cars**

Since its introduction of the aluminum low-pressure casting process in the late 1960s, ATS has been a player in the lightweight alloy wheel market. Today, the company is a primary supplier of original equipment to Audi, Mercedes, Volkswagen, and Porsche (whose 911 Turbo rides on hollow-spoke ATS alloy wheels). With 2,000 employees working in plants in Germany, Poland, and South Africa, ATS produces millions of wheels each year. Its current catalog lists a variety of wheels in the 15-to-22-inch range in silver and glossy finishes. ATS' motto is, "First class, out of one cast."

Axis

9046 Sorenson Ave.
Santa Fe Spring, CA 90670
562-906-9898
www.axiswheels.com

- **compacts**

- **cars**

- **trucks/SUVs**

Axis Sport Tuning features wheel designs to fit small to mid-size performance imports, domestic cars, and SUVs. Although the line runs from 17-to-22-inch diameters for 17 different designs, the company specializes in 19-inch wheel fitment for the Civic, Golf, and Jetta as well as the Mercedes C-class, 3-series BMW, and Audi in six different models. Axis produces its own wheels, which are manufactured using low-pressure casting methods for lighter weight. Popular models include the Speed Six, Ne-O, Vector, RT, Wheelsite Mesh II, and Mag-Lite.

Alegis (Photo Axis)

Bray (Photo Axis)

Hagen (Photo Axis)

Se7en (Photo Axis)

SLR (Photo Axis)

Touring (Photo Axis)

Autec

The Wheel Exchange
555 Dynamic Dr.
Garner, NC 27529
888-682-3129
www.thewheelexchange.com

- **cars**

According to its press material, Autec, which was founded in 1988, represents "the ultimate fusion of bold forward-moving design and precise German engineering." Its alloy wheels are manufactured by a low-pressure casting method, followed by a three-layer paint process.

Baccarat

866-222-2331
www.baccaratwheels.com

- **compacts**
- **cars**
- **trucks/SUVs**

Baccarat offers a line of luxury wheels with names like Kologne, Mirage, Link, and Allure. The top-line Allure is available in a 24-inch diameter, and features lip-mounted diamond-shaped inserts that can be ordered in chrome or gold finish.

Bazo

1315 John Reed Ct.
City of Industry, CA 91745
877-968-BAZO
www.bazowheels.com

- **cars**
- **trucks/SUVs**

With a line of 18-to-24-inch wheels named B1, B2, B3, etc., Bazo offers something to dress up a front- or rear-drive car or SUV/truck. According to company literature, "If you're a person who has got the future on your mind and at the same time you're taking the present by storm, then Bazo Wheels are you."

BBS

5320 BBS Dr.
Braselton, GA 30517
770-967-9848
www.bbs.com

- **compacts**

- **cars**

- **trucks/SUVs**

BBS is perhaps better known for its racing wheels than the product it makes for the street. This is especially true in Europe, where any pre-teen can tell you that Michael Schumacher has won four of his Formula 1 World Championships on BBS wheels. The Ferrari Challenge Cup cars all run BBS wheels. The German company currently offers three lines: Techno (featuring CH, RK, RKII, RC, and LeMans models), Classic (RZ, RX, RX II, and RS II) and Design (RW, RWII, Truck RW, and VZ). Applications include cars as inexpensive as the VW Golf, Ford Probe, Mitsubishi Eclipse, and Mini Cooper to the more lofty Mercedes SL, BMW 745i, and Porsche Carerra.

Billet Specialties

500 Shawmut Ave.
LaGrange, IL 60526
800-245-5382
www.billetspecialties.com

- **cars**

- **trucks/SUVs**

- **street rods**

- **vintage**

What started in 1985 as a small producer of billet aluminum accessories for the street rod crowd has blossomed into a giant in the industry. In addition to its brackets, mirrors, steering wheels, shift knobs, and air cleaners, Billet Specialties offers a line of show-quality wheels in the 15-to-22-inch range. They fit a variety of custom applications and come in a highly polished finish. A few models, such as the GTX and Cruise Line are available with the trendy "soft lip" treatment. Billet Specialties uses 6061-T6 high-grade aluminum.

Truck (Photo BBS)

GT (Photo BBS)

Challenge (Photo BBS)

Chicyane (Photo Billet Specialties)

GTX06 (Photo Billet Specialties)

Legacy (Photo Billet Specialties)

Rebel
(Photo Billet Specialties)

SLX45
(Photo Billet Specialties)

SLX37
(Photo Billet Specialties)

A (Photo Borbet)

A2 (Photo Borbet)

BS (Photo Borbet)

E (Photo Borbet)

M (Photo Borbet)

M2 (Photo Borbet)

R (Photo Borbet)

Borbet GmbH

The Tire Rack
7101 Vorden Parkway
South Bend, IN 46628
888-541-1777
www.borbet.com
www.tirerack.com

- **compacts**

- **cars**

Peter Wilhelm Borbet began manufacturing sand- and die-cast industrial parts in 1962. In 1977, his company produced its first light alloy wheels for cars and commercial vehicles. Today, the Borbet Group is a developer and supplier of light alloy wheels for automobile manufacturers such as AMG, Audi, BMW, DaimlerChrysler, Ford, GM, Peugeot, Porsche, Suzuki, Volvo, and Volkswagen. Borbet's various European factories produce more than two million wheels per year. Its 14-to-18-inch wheels come in a variety of designs in silver or painted finishes—most with machined lips.

T (Photo Borbet)

VS (Photo Borbet)

Boss

American Eagle Wheel
5780 Soestern Ct.
Chino, CA 91710
909-590-8828
www.aewheel.com

- **trucks/SUVs**

Boss Motorsport alloy wheels are produced by American Eagle Wheel in Chino, Calif., and measure from 18 to 22 inches in diameter. Models are simply named Boss 301, 303, 304, 305, and so on. American Eagle uses a "counter pressure-casting" manufacturing method for its Boss wheels. All are chrome-plated except for some versions of the 301.

3036 (Photo Brad Bowling)

3056 (Photo Brad Bowling)

with Vegas spinner (Photo Brad Bowling)

Boyd Coddington

861-A E. Lambert Rd.
La Habra, CA 90631
888-254-3400
www.billetwheel.com

- **compacts**
- **cars**
- **trucks/SUVs**
- **street rods**
- **vintage**

In the street rod world, the name Boyd Coddington is on par with royalty. The custom car builder is best known for his wild from-scratch creations like CadZilla, CheZoom, and The Boydster. The Coddington wheel line includes the 3/4 Ton, Butchin, Signature, Gotcha, Cast, and Exclusive series, which range in size from 14 to 22 inches. All are available in a highly polished finish that some enthusiasts feel is superior to chrome.

Boze

866-634-4626
www.bozeforged.com

- **compacts**
- **cars**
- **trucks/SUVs**
- **street rods**
- **vintage**

Nothing says "look at me" like a set of custom chrome wheels on your slammed SUV. Ranging in size from 17 to 22 inches, Boze billet aluminum wheels cover the spectrum of modern designs—from the elegant and simple Stixx and Stinger five-spokes to the busier Fusion, Dude, and Affliction. All Boze wheels feature "soft lip" construction.

Wedge (Photo Boze)

Fatal (Photo Boze)

Big Mamma (Photo Boze)

Branzach

16394 Downey Ave.
Paramount, CA 90723
866-278-7575
www.branzach.com

- **cars**

- **trucks/SUVs**

Branzach currently has three model lines—the BZ11, BZ15, and BZ 16—all available in standard or proprietary finishes. The company has introduced a unique black chrome finish, which it claims is an industry first. Achieving the black chrome look requires extra manufacturing steps after the chrome plating to achieve a very deep high-luster finish not currently available from other aftermarket wheel producers. In addition, Branzach has developed its own unique powder coat to create its very popular anthracite, bronze, and gold finishes. The company recently introduced black pearl, diamond black, and titanium gold to its line.

Breyton

The Tire Rack
7101 Vorden Parkway
South Bend, IN 46628
888-541-1777
www.tirerack.com

- **BMW cars**

- **BMW SUVs**

Breyton is a German aftermarket tuner that specializes in BMW applications. Its Magic, Magic Racing, and Magic Sport wheels epitomize the thin-spoke school of design, while the Emotion and Inspiration models are traditional five-spoke "stars." Sizes range from 17- to 22-inchers, with silver or chrome finishes.

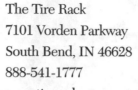

Emotion (Photo Tire Rack)

Magic Sport (Photo Tire Rack)

Vision (Photo Tire Rack)

BSA

4690 NW 167th St.
Opa Locka, FL 33054
305-620-RIMS
www.bsaalloywheels.com

- cars
- compacts
- trucks/SUVs

BSA's extensive catalog of alphanumeric-named wheels (225c, 215a, 233s, etc.) runs the gamut from the classic five-spoke star design to the thin-spoke, super-light look. Wheels are sized from 14 to 20 inches and come in silver, painted, polished, or chrome finishes.

Budnik

15251 Pipeline Ln.
Huntington Beach, CA 92649
714-892-1932
www.budnik.com

- cars
- compacts
- trucks/SUVs

From sizes 14 to 22, Budnik produces a full range of designs for any four-wheeled vehicle. Each wheel begins life as a heat-treated forged billet center, which is then machined front and back for a show-quality appearance before being polished to a mirror finish. Budnik currently offers five distinct series of wheels—the X, S, HDX, XX, and Fat Lip. Its "fat lip" is an evolution of the currently popular soft lip, whereby the usually flat outermost part of the rim is given a rounded appearance.

Carlsson

The Tire Rack
7101 Vorden Parkway
South Bend, IN 46628
888-541-1777
www.tirerack.com

- Mercedes cars
- Mercedes SUVs

Andreas and Rolfe Hartge, whose thriving BMW aftermarket performance parts and tuning business was well established by 1989, started Carlsson Autotechnik to perform the same type of modifications to Mercedes-Benz automobiles. As with the Hartge product line, Carlsson offers its customers aerodynamic body pieces, suspension upgrades, and high-performance engine installations, as well as a line of stylish alloy wheels. The 17-to-19-inch rims come in silver, chrome, or painted finishes.

Center Line

13521 Freeway Dr.
Santa Fe Springs, CA 90670
800-345-8671
www.centerlinewheels.com

- cars
- compacts
- trucks/SUVs

Founded in 1970 by Ray Lipper, one of the pioneers in the aftermarket wheel industry, Center Line is today one of the largest wheel makers in the United States. From drag races to car shows, there is a Center Line alloy wheel for every application, with its latest catalog displaying hundreds of models. Its Millennium and H/T Comp series cover the truck and SUV market, while the Dominator, Orbital, Phantom, Sundance, and others fill the bill for car fitment. Racing wheels, once Center Line's bread and butter and best form of advertising, are represented by a series of 15-to-17-inch rims available in various levels of polish.

Comet (Photo Brad Bowling)

Outlaw (Photo Brad Bowling)

Telstar (Photo Brad Bowling)

Colorado Custom

363 Jefferson St.,
Ste. 101
Ft Collins, CO 80525
877-805-0659, www.coloradocustom.com

- **cars**

- **compacts**

- **trucks/SUVs**

- **street rods**

Manes Machine & Engineering, a company that provides precision-machined products to the aerospace industry under private contracts, began in 1982 in Corona, Calif., then moved to Ft. Collins, Colo., in 1992. Two years later, it entered the automotive aftermarket with the Colorado Custom line of alloy wheels. Many of the company's 14-to-22-inch wheels are named after towns or cities in its home state, which explains the Leadville, Arvada, Steamboat, Telluride, Aurora, and Buffalo Creek models. As one would expect from a firm with ties to aerospace, browsing through its catalog proves that creativity of design is not in short supply with Colorado Custom. In addition to the standard five-spoke, thin-spoke, and blade designs, the CC lineup includes wheels inspired by fire and other natural forces.

Concept Neeper

MHT Luxury Alloy Wheels
6907 Marlin Cir.
La Palma, CA 90623
310-783-0407
www.neeper.com

- **cars**

- **compacts**

- **trucks/SUVs**

- **street rods**

The man behind the name, Mark Neeper, is an automotive conceptual artist whose ideas were turned into metal starting in the mid-1990s. Not only do Neeper's chrome wheels occupy the plus-size end of the scale in the 17-to-20-inch range for cars and 20-to-23-inch spectrum for trucks (16s for dually applications), but they are some of the most unusual and eye-catching designs on the street. Model names such as Monsta, Megga, Klutch, and Retro belie the fact that Mr. Neeper is having way too much fun creating the wheels that bear his name.

Isis (Photo Brad Bowling)

Cragar

2233 E. Philadelphia St.
Ontario, CA 91761
909-947-1831
www.cragar.com

- **cars**

- **compacts**

- **trucks/SUVs**

- **vintage**

Founded in 1930 by Crane Gartz and Harlan Fengler for the purposes of manufacturing automotive cylinder heads, Cragar (from "Cra"ne and "Gar"tz) did not become a producer of wheels until 1964. That first S/S model—a five-spoke "mag"—caught the imagination of the racing and custom car world and set the standard for all aftermarket wheels to come. Today, an updated version of the S/S (still hot as a "retro" model) is in the Cragar catalog along with designs no one could have dreamed of in 1964, with trendy names like Tease, Edge, Boost, and E-Tune in diameters ranging from 16 to 22 inches—most from cast aluminum.

S/S (Photo Brad Bowling)

Tru-Spoke (Photo Brad Bowling)

CSA

25-47 Cheviot Rd.
Salisbury South Australia 5108
(08) 8282 3600
www.mullins.com.au

- **compacts**

- **cars**

- **trucks/SUVs**

This Down Under wheel manufacturer has a line of 13- to 18-inch alloy wheels for a variety of cars and trucks. With names like Prowler, Predator, Gladiator, and Reactor, it's easy to remember that these are the folks who gave us Mad Max.

Davin

220 West Exchange St.
Ste. 107
Providence, RI 02903
401-273-8041
www.davinwheels.com

- **compacts**

- **cars**

- **trucks/SUVs**

When David Fowlkes created a class project for the Minneapolis College of Art and Design in 1990, he didn't realize it would turn out to be the "next big thing" in the aftermarket wheel world. In January 2001, Davin Wheels (a conglomeration of Fowlkes and partners Henry Seemore and Ian Hardman) introduced the first example of spinning rim and freespin technology—the Revolution 1.0—at the LA Auto Show. Composed of a base wheel and a freespinning facade, these incredibly expensive rims give the illusion of being stationary while the vehicle is moving and vice versa. Ranging in size from 19 to 24 inches in diameter, Davin's spinning wheels have been phenomenally popular since introduction with hip-hop artists, sports stars, and high-profile actors.

Detata

Wheel Country
888-810-6247

- **compacts**

- **cars**

- **trucks/SUVs**

The Detata Alloy Wheels lineup currently includes diameters ranging from 16 to 22 inches. Chrome, chrome and chrome are the finishes available on the Detata models, which include the Profiler, Allure, Essex, Ridge, Boxer, Traxx, and Rallye.

Essex (Photo Brad Bowling)

T108 (Photo Brad Bowling)

D.O.A.

6907 Marlin Circle
LaPalma, CA 90623
866-880-4362
www.doawheels.com

- **trucks/SUVs**

Now here's a company that's not afraid to use morbid imagery to sell an automotive product! D.O.A.'s Web site features a graphic with the greenish, upturned feet of what can only be assumed to be a corpse. Its three models—named Toe Tag, Flatliner, and Penalty—inhabit the super-size end of the wheel spectrum for trucks and SUVs at 20 to 22 inches in diameter.

Drïv

MHT Luxury Alloy Wheels
6907 Marlin Cir.
La Palma, CA 90623
310-783-0407
www.drivwheels.com

- **compacts**
- **cars**
- **trucks/SUVs**

Barricade, Torq, Plague, Mach 5, Cardiac, Paranoia, and Debut make up the Drïv line of 16-to-23-inch mirror-finish chrome wheels.

Eagle

American Eagle Wheel
5780 Soestern Ct.
Chino, CA 91710
909-590-8828
www.aewheel.com

- **cars**
- **compacts**
- **trucks/SUVs**

Eagle alloy wheels are produced by American Eagle Wheel in Chino, Calif., and measure from 15 to 22 inches in diameter. The catalog is heavy on applications for rear-drive cars, SUVs, and front-drive compacts. American Eagle uses a "counter pressure-casting" manufacturing method for its Eagle wheels. All are chrome-plated or polished.

0776 (Photo Brad Bowling)

1189 (Photo Brad Bowling)

1776 (Photo Brad Bowling)

289 (Photo Brad Bowling)

071 (Photo Brad Bowling)

Egoist

16394 Downey Ave.
Paramount, CA 90723
866-278-7575
www.branzach.com

- **Lexus GS and IS cars**

Designed and manufactured in Japan and marketed through Branzach Corporation in the U.S., Egoist wheels are offered exclusively for Lexus GS and IS models. The line currently consists of two models—the 18-inch Egoist and 19-inch Perfect Queen.

Elite

MHT Luxury Alloy Wheels
6907 Marlin Cir.
La Palma, CA 90623
866-22ELITE
www.elitealloys.com

- **cars**

- **compacts**

- **trucks/SUVs**

Elite products are produced by the MHT Alloy Wheels group. The line runs from 15 to 23 inches in diameter, with a heavy emphasis on mirror-quality chrome finishes. Barb, Amp, Impeller, and Powerglide are some of the models in the Elite family.

EMO

12850 Moore St.
Cerritos, CA 90703
877-968-7366
www.emowheels.com

- **compacts**

- **cars**

- **trucks/SUVs**

EMO was derived from "Eminent Magnum Opus," which means "Magnificent Work of Art," according to the company Web site. The site doubles as an online store,

where enthusiasts can purchase simply named 804, 805, 808, or 811 wheels for an impressive variety of American and imported cars (in 15-to-18 inch diameters) and 515, 610, and 868 wheels for trucks (15 to 20 inches).

Enkei

800-843-9145
www.enkei.com

- **compacts**

- **cars**

- **trucks/SUVs**

Enkei's half-century in the aftermarket wheel business has earned the company a reputation for designing innovative and high-quality products. Brevet, Enkei's newest line of chrome alloy wheels for luxury SUVs, includes the 20- and 22-inch Justice five-spoke, 18- and 20-inch six-spoke Reign, 17- and 18-inch Liberty, 17-to-20-inch five-spoke Victory, 17-to-20-inch six-spoke Valor, and 17-to-18-inch Silverstar—all finished in mirror-quality chrome. That's just one line; the Milano, EX, Tuning, Sport, Truck, and Exclusives cover dozens more designs for just about any vehicle type.

CTM-3
(Photo Brad Bowling)

Wun-Gun
(Photo Brad Bowling)

Epic

9067 S. Reyes Ave.
Rancho Dominguez, CA 90221
800-959-1969
www.epicwheels.com

- **compacts**
- **cars**
- **trucks/SUVs**

Epic has a line of chromed alloy wheels in the popular 16-to-20-inch diameter range for cars and 16-to-24-inch spectrum for SUVs and trucks. Models include the Triad, Blix, Miamits, Stryke, Claw, and Gladiator.

Epic (Photo Brad Bowling)

WLC (Photo Brad Bowling)

Equus

800-327-1144
www.equuswheels.com

- **compacts**
- **cars**
- **trucks/SUVs**

Equus wheels tend to be on the large side, with diameters ranging from 16 inches to a whopping 26 inches. These gigantic chrome or silver rims are available for rear-wheel, front-wheel, and all-wheel drive applications.

308
(Photo Brad Bowling)

EVO

933 Mulberry St.
Kansas City, MO 64101
866-753-4272
www.weldevo.com

- **cars**
- **trucks/SUVs**

After earning its reputation as a producer of quality competition steel and alloy wheels, Weld Racing introduced its new line of EVO forged aluminum one-piece wheels in 1999. Under eight million pounds of pressure, EVO wheels are pressed from 6061 aircraft-grade aluminum after being heated to 800 degrees—a process that literally squeezes the air out of the alloy for more consistent strength. As the EVO wheel moves through Weld's 87,000-square-foot manufacturing facility, it is robot polished before succumbing to a six-layer chrome finish in a 36-tank process. Due to the diligence of this system, EVO guarantees its chrome finishes for five years. EVO wheels are available for Mercedes, Lexus, and Corvette as well as trucks and SUVs. Sizes run from 16 to 22 inches.

Axis SL
(Photo Tire Rack)

Slingblade 6
(Photo Tire Rack)

Velociti 8
(Photo Tire Rack)

Factory Reproductions

1440 W. Brooks St.
Ontario, CA 91762
800-824-2676
www.factoryreproductions.com

- **compacts**

- **cars**

- **trucks/SUVs**

The name of the company says it all. If you want to upgrade your BMW, Corvette, Mustang, Lightning, Camaro, IROC, Lexus, Impala, or SUV to a higher level of factory-style rim, Factory Reproductions probably has it in stock. In some cases, the company offers sizes and offsets that were not available from the factory.

IROC SUV
(Photo Factory Reproductions)

Ford F-150 Harley
(Photo Factory Reproductions)

Lexus LS 430
(Photo Factory Reproductions)

SSR SUV 6-Spoke
(Photo Factory Reproductions)

BMW M3
(Photo Factory Reproductions)

BMW Parallel Spoke
(Photo Factory Reproductions)

Corvette ZR1
(Photo Factory Reproductions)

Corvette Z06
(Photo Factory Reproductions)

Falken

10404 Sixth St.
Rancho Cucamonga, CA 91730
909-466-1116
www.falkentire.com

- **compacts**

- **cars**

- **trucks/SUVs**

Although better known for its line of high-performance, all-season and light-duty truck tires, Falken now makes a line of 17- to 23-inch alloy wheels on which to mount them. Its Torque 5 and Circuit Spec wheels for cars come in 17-, 18-, and 19-inch diameters and are available in gunmetal or silver finishes. Roid and Spine are the 20-, 22-, and 23-inch truck wheels, available only in chrome.

Focal

6300 Valley View Ave.
Buena Park, CA 90620
704-994-1444
www.ultrawheel.com

- **compacts**

- **cars**

- **trucks/SUVs**

Focal alloy rims are made by the folks at Ultra, which has been manufacturing custom wheels for cars, trucks, and vans for nearly 20 years from its Buena Park, Calif., plant. Its current Focal line comes in diameters 17 to 19 inches and include options for chrome, silver, or Ultra finish.

163 (Photo Brad Bowling)

Fondmetal

Via Bergamo, 4
24050 Palosco (Bg) Italy
+39 035 845130
www.fondmetal.com

- **compacts**

- **cars**

Fondmetal is an Italian company with a line of alloy wheels in the 13-to-18-inch range, but the name is more closely associated with the ultra-high technologies it has developed for Formula 1 racing in Europe. Fondmetal performs aerodynamic research and suspension development for a number of championship teams. Its wheels are available in a natural aluminum finish.

Foose Design

2610 Columbia St.
Torrance, CA 90503
877-963-6673
www.foosedesignwheels.com

- **street rods**

- **trucks/SUVs**

Chip Foose is widely recognized as one of America's top hot rod designers. Responsible for the biggest evolutionary leaps made in hot rodding during the past 15 years, Foose has won five "Street Rod of the Year" awards, four "America's Most Beautiful Roadster" awards and is the youngest person ever inducted into the Hot Rod Hall of Fame. Foose's wheel line currently includes 12 one- and multi-piece models, with names like Spank, Nitrous Thrust, and Altered. Wheels run the gamut from 15 to 24 inches in diameter, and all are chrome finished. Foose also has dually wheels for people who just haven't spent enough money on their tow rig already.

Spank (Photo Brad Bowling)

Ford Racing

The Tire Rack
7101 Vorden Parkway
South Bend, IN 46628
888-541-1777
www.tirerack.com
www.fordracing.com

- **compacts**

- **cars**

- **trucks/SUVs**

Ford Racing wheels—primarily for Mustangs and SVT Cobras—can be bought through various certified Ford dealerships and other retail and catalog outlets.

Bullitt (Photo Tire Rack)

SVT Cobra (Photo Tire Rack)

SVT Lightning (Photo Tire Rack)

Genx

4201 S. Market Ct. #A
Sacramento, CA 95834
916-920-3220
www.genxwheels.com

- **cars**

- **trucks/SUVs**

Genx wheels occupy the "how big is too big?" end of the spectrum; its Desperado, Exxen, Titan, and Xtek measuring between 19 and 23 inches in diameter. The wheels are one-piece aluminum construction and are available only in a highly polished chrome.

Gianelle

866-GIANELLE
www.gianelledesigns.com

- **cars**

- **trucks/SUVs**

Gianelle's 17-to-20-inch Flush and Twin models are for cars; the 20-to-23-inch five-spoke Split is designed for trucks and SUVs. The Oval runs 18 to 20 inches as a car wheel and plumps to 22 inches for SUVs. All Gianelle wheels are available in silver or chrome finishes.

Giovanna

800-307-8708
www.giovannawheels.com

- **cars**

- **trucks/SUVs**

Giovanna sells a beautiful line of alloy wheels in the popular 17-to-23-inch range. Its Eesen, Nagano, Drama, Corsica, Anzio, Modena, and Attack are available in either chrome or silver finishes.

Gram Lights

9921 Jordan Circle
P.O. Box 4025
Santa Fe Springs, CA 90670
562-946-6820
www.mackinindustries.com
www.rayswheels.co.jp

- **compacts**

- **cars**

Gram Lights wheels are aimed squarely at the exploding JDM (Japanese Domestic Market) audience on the West Coast. Its line of super-light alloy 14-to-19-inch wheels are made for Nissan's Skyline, Fairlady Z, Silvia, Toyota's Celica, the Mazda RX-7, Mitsubishi Lancer, and Subaru Impreza/WRX. The company also produces an extensive line of body kits for those cars.

57C
(Photo Mackin Industries)

57F
(Photo Mackin Industries)

57 Pro
(Photo Mackin Industries)

Halibrand

620-326-2111
www.halibrand.com

- **cars**

- **street rods**

- **vintage**

In 1946 former World War II aircraft mechanic Ted Halibrand single-handedly began the lightweight performance wheel industry when he cast an experimental set of rims from high-strength magnesium. Halibrand's firsthand knowledge of the racing world and enthusiasm for innovation led him to create wheels and other equipment that helped win many Indianapolis 500 races and secure world speed records. Ford fans will no doubt remember the stylish Halibrand "mags" (a shorthand reference to their magnesium content) that adorned Carroll Shelby's 289 and 427 Cobras and GT-40 race cars. Because of their success on the track, Halibrand wheels found their way on to thousands of street rods and custom cars during the last 50 years. Today, Halibrand offers eight

aluminum wheel designs—four cast and four machined—including the Speedway, Kidney Bean, Sweet Swirl, and Sprint.

Hartge

Dazz Motorsport
5121 Commerce Drive
Baldwin Park, CA 91706-1451
626-962-0033
www.dazzmotorsports.com

- **BMW cars**

- **BMW SUVs**

What started as a BMW repair garage in Germany in 1971 has evolved into the world's premier tuner of Bavaria's famous driving machines. Hartge offers BMW owners suspension, bodywork, exhaust, and aerodynamic upgrades. Its Nova 3, Nova 5, and Nova 7 wheels come in 18-, 19-, and 20-inch diameters, respectively. All three can be finished in silver or chrome. The Classic comes in 18- and 19-inch sizes, although there is a 22-incher for the X5 sport utility vehicle and 7-series sedan.

High Impact

PO Box 2089
Shingle Springs, CA 95682
888-898-4331
www.high-impact.net

- **4x4s**

High Impact Beadlock Wheels come in 15- and 17-inch diameters only. They are not for the "look at me" luxury wheel crowd—more like the "look out, I'm driving into a ravine" rock-climbing type. Wheels are available in all-steel or aluminum-and-steel construction. A "beadlock" is a device that clamps the tire bead in place using mechanical force rather than air pressure. It holds the bead firmly in place even at extremely low air pressure. High Impact wheels have 32-bolt locks on each of its rims, and can accommodate up to 44-inch tires.

Daytona
(Photo High Impact)

Baja
(Photo High Impact)

8-Lug Modular
(Photo High Impact)

Camo Modular
(Photo High Impact)

Chrome
(Photo High Impact)

Monster
(Photo High Impact)

2453 Cades Way
Bldg. A
Vista, CA 92083
760-598-1960
www.hrewheels.com

- **cars**

- **compacts**

- **trucks/SUVs**

HRE specializes in custom forged aluminum wheels for high-performance and luxury vehicles. Each model in its line of three-piece wheels can be manufactured to customer specifications. Ranging in diameter from 16 to 20 inches (car) or 18 to 24 inches (SUV), HRE's wheels are available in high polish, custom paint, brushed/clearcoat, charcoal paint, and anodized black and silver paint finishes. For the show-conscious buyer, the 540R series incorporates a hidden valve stem.

446R
(Photo HRE)

540R
(Photo HRE)

841R
(Photo HRE)

Ice Metal

www.wheelpros.com

- **cars**
- **compacts**
- **trucks/SUVs**

Ice Metal is a line of one-piece alloy wheels available in 16-to-20-inch diameters. Models 887, 882, 885, and 884 are designed for rear-drive applications, while front-drivers can be fitted with the 881, 883, or 886—all in mirror-like chrome.

ICW Racing

www.icwracing.com

- **cars**
- **compacts**
- **tuners**

ICW Racing specializes in fitments for today's hot import and domestic tuner market. ICW offers more than 20 styles in a variety of finishes, including silver, white, the new hyper silver, and chrome plated finishes.

ICW-1 (Photo Brad Bowling)

ICW-2 (Photo Brad Bowling)

Intro

10931 Court Ave.
Stanton, CA 90680
714-963-6803
www.introwheels.com

- **cars**
- **trucks/SUVs**
- **vintage**

Intro billet aluminum wheels range in size from 15 to 22 inches, with all exposed surfaces receiving a high level of polish. Several Intro models look like new twists on classic designs, like the Vista—a five-spoker with a passing resemblance to Cragar's original S/S—and the high-tech Smoothie, which brings the lake racer look into the 21st century. The Vista is also available with Intro's own satin suede finish.

Ion Alloy

Wheel Country
888-810-6247
www.ionalloy.com

- **cars**
- **trucks/SUVs**

Ion Alloy wheels are produced by The Wheel Group, which also owns Bacarrat, Veloché, Mazzi, Sacchi, Detroit, and Dip. With names like Type 88, Type 111, and Type 128, the chrome wheels run as large as 20-inch diameters.

Kaizer

SK Performance
15515 SE Honeysuckle Way
Clackamas, OR 97015
503-232-2058
www.skperformance.com

- **cars**
- **compacts**
- **trucks/SUVs**

Kaizer front-drive wheel models include the Circus 2, Mirage, PHX 2, PHX 3, and Spade, available in a range from 17 to 20 inches in diameter. SUV wheels run from 18 to 23 inches and features names like Ennocent, Guilty 2, and Elude.

Kaotik

MHT Luxury Alloy Wheels
6907 Marlin Cir.
La Palma, CA 90623
800-648-7467
www.kaotikstreetalloys.com

- **cars**

- **trucks/SUVs**

Passion, Z-5, Z-6, Stinger 3, Slide, Scorch, and Parole make up the Kaotik Street Alloys product line. Sizes range from 17 to 24, and wheels are available in any finish you want as long as you want chrome.

Katana

707 N. Barranca Ave.
Unit 6
Covina, CA 91723
877-44WHEEL
www.katanawheels.com

- **cars**

- **trucks/SUVs**

Katana has been manufacturing alloy wheels for cars and SUVs since the mid-1990s. Its current line of 15-to-22-inch models includes the five-spoke Inspire, split six-spoke K-6, and super-thin-spoke Ducati. Chrome, silver, white, and gunmetal are the finishes Katana offers throughout its line.

KMC

1455 Columbia Ave.
Riverside, CA 92507
800-864-4387, www.kmcwheels.com

- **compact cars**

- **cars**

- **trucks/SUVs**

KMC covers just about everything that's hot right now. The truck/SUV crowd is bound to find something it likes in the 15-to-23-inch range with the Bofa, Dupe, Madness, Venom, Hellion, Picasso, Clocker, Zipper, and Rooster, to name a few—finishes include chrome or polished. The front-drive market is served by the 15-to-20-inch Floss, Spawn, Gnome, Unit, and Guido in chrome or polished finishes. Tuner kids can choose from the 17-to-19-inch Wizdom, Suicide, or RPM line in chrome or silver. Even folks looking to dress up dually trucks have the Rally, Adrenaline, Relic, and Talon as options—all in 16-inch form with a polished finish.

KMC (Photo Brad Bowling)

750 (Photo Brad Bowling)

Ace (Photo KMC)

Slinger (Photo KMC)

Tempest (Photo KMC)

Venom (Photo Brad Bowling)

König

121 Express Street
Plainview, NY 11803
516-822-5700
www.konigwheels.com

- **cars**

- **compacts**

- **trucks/SUVs**

König was established in 1983 as a subsidiary of the New York-based Pan Mar import/export company. Its philosophy/motto/ad line is "Style is Everything." One look through the König catalog reveals the company does not take its mission lightly. Beautifully styled models with names like GreenLight Silver, Blatant Carbon, Rewind Gold, Absolute Platinum, and Appeal Opal indicate why König has a loyal following among the trendy compact car and truck/SUV show crowd. Wheels range from 15 to 20 inches in diameter.

Drone
(Photo König)

Prophet
(Photo König)

Theory
(Photo König)

Kosei

The Tire Rack
7101 Vorden Parkway
South Bend, IN 46628
888-541-1777
www.tirerack.com

- **compact cars**

- **cars**

From the design studios of the Pacific Rim come the diverse styles of Kosei. The 15-to-17-inch lightweight K1 wheels are available in white, anthracite, or silver, while the 17- and 18-inch Sniper are only offered in silver.

K1 (Photo Tire Rack)

Kronix

23705 Via Del Rio
Yorba Linda, CA 92887
866-4KRONIX
www.kronixwheels.com

- **cars**

- **trucks/SUVs**

Ekko, Insignia, and Biohazard are the three models offered by the Kronix Exotic Wheel Concepts company. Each of the chromed 17-to-20-inch wheels are styled using harsh geometric forms and sharp edges. If loud music and explosions figure into your wheel-buying decisions, check out the Kronix video on the company's Web site.

Lexani

23705 Via Del Rio
Yorba Linda, CA 92887
800-833-9700
www.lexani.com

- **cars**

- **trucks/SUVs**

According to its press material, "Lexani toys with genetic engineering to originate new life in every creation." A few wheels in Lexani's range of 17-to-24-inchers incorporate a lot of the less popular geometric designs and knife-sharp edges, resulting in models that recall Ben-Hur's racing chariot. The company definitely takes its creativity to heart, though; some models, like the NV, Synergy, and Marqi don't look like anything else on the road. From the same company that brings us Kronix wheels, Lexani also has a Web site heavy on video, music, and scantily clad women.

Lorenzo

1455 Columbia Ave.
Riverside, CA 92507
800-864-4387
www.lorenzowheels.com

- **compact cars**

- **cars**

- **trucks/SUVs**

Lorenzo wheels are aimed squarely at the Gigantor-size crowd, with rims measuring 18 to 20 inches in diameter and chrome plated over every square inch. The company's line of one-piece alloy wheels feature a Lorenzo exclusive—Superlip construction that results in a deep rivet molding for the look of a two-piece rim. Models currently include the easy-to-remember Lo 1, Lo 2, Lo 3, through Lo 6 with applications covering the high-end luxury cars and SUVs.

Lo4 (Photo Lorenzo)

Lo5 (Photo Lorenzo)

Lo6 (Photo Lorenzo)

Löwenhart

Dazz Motorsport
5121 Commerce Drive
Baldwin Park, CA 91706-1451
626-962-0033
www.dazzmotorsports.com

- **cars**

- **SUVs**

Löwenhart produces a line of high-dollar multi-piece chrome, silver, and polished wheels for Corvettes, Mercedes-Benzes, and other passenger cars, as well as for SUVs. Models include the 18-to-21-inch LDS, 24-inch LT6, 22-to-23-inch LD6, 18-to-20-inch BR5, and 18-23-inch LD1. Löwenhart also produces some unintentionally amusing company literature, with comments such as, "Its feeling of presence is thoroughly pervaded with self-assurance," and "The excitement of getting your hands on it, that is the assence [sic] of Löwenhart."

L-Sportline

Dazz Motorsport
5121 Commerce Dr.
Baldwin Park, CA 91706-1451
626-472-7160
www.lsportline.com

- **Lexus cars**

If BMW and Mercedes have their own specialty tuners devoted to the marques, someone figured a popular, refined nameplate like Lexus should enjoy such enthusiasm as well. In addition to its suspension, exhaust, and aerodynamic improvements, L-Sportline offers a line of upscale alloy wheels for customers who want their Lexus cars to stand out from the crowd. Named, simply enough, Model 1, Model 2, Model 3, and Model 4, the 18-to-20-inch wheels are available in various combinations of chrome and silver. Model 3 and a version of Model 4 are one-piece rims, while Model 1, Model 2 and an alternate version of Model 4 are multi-piece wheels.

MAE

Dazz Motorsport
5121 Commerce Drive
Baldwin Park, CA 91706-1451
626-962-0033
www.dazzmotorsports.com

- **Mercedes-Benz cars**

The MAE Crown Jewel I, offered only in silver, is a one-piece alloy wheel available in 18- and 19-inch applications for late-model Mercedes automobiles. The Crown Jewel III is a multi-piece Mercedes aftermarket wheel available in 19- and 20-inch chrome versions. Both Crown Jewels, manufactured by O.Z. of Italy, hold design patents.

Maido

Dazz Motorsport
5121 Commerce Dr.
Baldwin Park, CA 91706-1451
626-480-0243
www.maidowheels.com

- **cars**
- **trucks/SUVs**

Maido currently offers eight models of chrome or silver 18-to-24-inch wheels. The GR5, CR5, BR3, LS5, and MD1 are for passenger car applications; the SD6, LS6, and MS5 are for SUVs. Most are of multi-piece construction.

Maxxim

121 Express Street
Plainview, NY 11803
800-501-5567 ext. 9001
www.maxximwheels.com

- **cars**
- **compacts**
- **trucks/SUVs**

Maxxim wheels are imported to the U.S. by König. The line includes more than two dozen styles for cars and SUVs, including the Baang, Oxygene, Def-Con6 Carbon, and Rumor (14 to 18 inches for cars), and Badda Bing and Hyadoin (18 to 20 inches for SUVs). Available finishes include graphite, silver, and chrome.

Creed (Photo Maxxim)

Eracer (Photo Maxxim)

Harpoon (Photo Maxxim)

Mirage (Photo Maxxim)

Oxygene (Photo Maxxim)

Maya

Dazz Motorsport
5121 Commerce Dr.
Baldwin Park, CA 91706-1451
626-962-0033
www.mayawheels.com

- **cars**

According to the company, Maya wheels mate multi-piece form and function while not sacrificing strength or durability. Four models—the BTC, DTM, DTS, and TTS—are offered in silver or chrome. The STM comes in "hyper black." All models except the BTC have polished lips. Diameters range from 18 to 22 inches.

Milanni

800-453-9842
www.milanni.com

- **cars**

- **trucks/SUVs**

Milanni is a new company specializing in the super-size segment of the aftermarket wheel industry, with chromed wheels ranging from 20 to 24 inches in diameter.

Mille Miglia

The Tire Rack
7101 Vorden Parkway
South Bend, IN 46628
888-541-1777
www.tirerack.com
www.millemiglia.co.uk

- **compact cars**

- **cars**

- **trucks/SUVs**

Mille Miglia wheels are produced by Due Emme MilleMiglia in Brescia, Italy—an area that has long specialized in the casting of aluminum. Brescia also holds the distinction of being the starting point for the 1,000-mile road race through Italy (last run at competitive speeds in 1957) known locally as the "Mille Miglia." Due Emme MilleMiglia is a self-contained business, with its 150 employees overseeing every aspect of wheel production—from initial mould construction and purchase of raw materials to production, packaging, and shipping. As one might expect from a company with such close ties to Italy's racing history, its wheels are beautifully designed and feature names like Avia, Bello, Impera, Mesa, and Emotion. They range from 16 to 20 inches, span the spectrum of styles—including a white five-spoke wearing a yellow cap called "Daisy White"—and can be had in chrome, silver, or painted finishes.

Cello
(Photo Tire Rack)

EV-S
(Photo Tire Rack)

Illuminati
(Photo Mizati)

Lotus
(Photo Mizati)

Manza
(Photo Mizati)

Wrath
(Photo Mizati)

Mizati

16122 Orange Ave.
Paramount, CA 90723
562-531-8886
www.mizatiwheels.com

- **compacts**

- **cars**

- **trucks/SUVs**

Mizati's imaginatively named Manza, Ace of Diamonds, Shifter I, Illuminati, Lotus, Wrath of Envy, Apollo 6, and Shifter II wheels run from 18 to 22 inches in diameter. They are available in both standard and positive offset, with some models offering an extra-cost gold-plated center cap.

MKW

1315 John Reed Ct.
City of Industry, CA 91745
800-234-5314
www.mkwheel.com

- **compacts**

- **cars**

- **trucks/SUVS**

MKW makes a line of large-scale chromed alloy wheels in the 17-to-24-inch range—all in mirror-polish chrome.

Ace of Diamonds
(Photo Mizati)

Apollo 6 (Photo Mizati)

MK-11
(Photo Brad Bowling)

Moda

The Tire Rack
7101 Vorden Parkway
South Bend, IN 46628
888-541-1777
www.tirerack.com

- **compacts**

- **cars**

- **trucks/SUVs**

Moda is another line of wheels bred on the race tracks of the world. Its R-1 through R-8 and F5 wheels measure 15 to 20 inches in diameter and are available in painted silver or polished stainless finish.

F5
(Photo Tire Rack)

R3
(Photo Tire Rack)

R8
(Photo Tire Rack)

MOMO

MOMO Automotive Accessories
25471 Arctic Ocean Dr.
Lake Forest, CA 92630
949-380-7556
www.momo.it

- **cars**

- **trucks/SUVs**

Few names carry as much panache in the automotive aftermarket industry as Momo, an Italian company that was born from a single good design. When founder Giampiero Moretti gave Formula One racer John Surtees one of his new steering wheels, the Ferrari driver liked it so much that his factory sponsor was the first customer when MOMO (short for Moretti-Monza) began production in 1966. Eventually, MOMO branched into racing and road wheels for cars, which have become as popular and revered as its original product line. Its 15-to-23-inch rims—available in silver, anthracite, black matte, shiny black, chrome, or white—are beautifully styled. Some, like the Quasar 2, are as smooth and purposeful as a well-worn rock; others, like the more elaborate six-spoke Racer Evo, are proof that Italy still gives birth to the great automotive designers.

Motegi

www.1010tires.com

- **cars**

- **compacts**

Motegi alloys run from 14 to 18 inches and are a hit with the compact car and tuner crowd. Available in white, silver, gunmetal, "super" silver, and chrome, Motegi's line of wheels offers several beautiful thin-spoke designs—the better to see those expensive aftermarket disc brake calipers and rotors on your Civic!

207 (Photo Brad Bowling)

ROJA (Photo Brad Bowling)

MSR

American Eagle Wheel
5780 Soestern Ct.
Chino, CA 91710
909-590-8828
www.aewheel.com

- **cars**

- **compacts**

- **trucks/SUVs**

MSR alloy wheels are produced by American Eagle Wheel in Chino, Calif., and measure from 16 to 20 inches in diameter. American Eagle uses a "counter pressure-casting" manufacturing method for its MSR wheels. All models are available in silver, chrome, or polished finishes.

MSR-1 (Photo Brad Bowling)

MSR-2 (Photo Brad Bowling)

MVR

Dazz Motorsport
5121 Commerce Dr.
Baldwin Park, CA 91706-1451
626-962-0033
www.dazzmotorsport.com

- **BMW cars**

- **BMW SUVs**

MVR offers a single-piece silver or chrome wheel for BMW cars or SUVs called the Magnum. It is available in 17- or 19-inch diameters.

Niche

MHT Luxury Alloy Wheels
6907 Marlin Cir.
La Palma, CA 90623
800-600-3271
www.nicheroadwheels.com

- **compacts**

- **cars**

- **trucks/SUVs**

F-16, B.C., Orca, Flash, Britaine, Spitfire, Max, and Throttle make up the Niche line of 16-to-22-inch mirror-finish chrome wheels.

Throttle (Photo Brad Bowling)

Niche 1 (Photo Brad Bowling)

NITRO

Golden Apple Corporation
3532 Arden Road
Hayward, CA 94545
510-780-9800
www.adrwheels.com

- **trucks/SUVs**

- **off-road**

NITRO is a line of 15- to 17-inch truck wheels. Designs include several takes on the classic five-spoke (NIT-02, NIT-03 and NIT-10) as well as a wilder, multi-spoke design (NIT-08). Finishes include natural silver or chrome.

NIT-06 (Photo Brad Bowling)

NIT-07 (Photo NITRO)

NIT-10 (Photo NITRO)

Oettinger

The Wheel Exchange
555 Dynamic Dr.
Garner, NC 27529
888-682-3129
www.thewheelexchange.com

- **Audi cars**

- **Volkswagen cars**

Oettinger Technik GmbH is a German aftermarket parts producer specializing in Audi and Volkswagen cars. Along with its aerodynamic body kits, suspension enhancements, stereo upgrades, and Autobahn-legal driving lights is a line of high-performance alloy wheels.

Omega

Custom Wheels Direct
10221 Prospect
Santee, CA 92071
619-448-2560
www.customwheelsdirect.com

- **compacts**

- **cars**

- **trucks/SUVs**

Omega wheels are produced by Atlantic Wholesalers. Wheels range from 17 to 24 inches in diameter, with 26-inch Zab Judah Hypnotic and Zab Judah 2 models promised soon. The Omega line features spinners and non-spinners—all covered liberally in chrome. The high-end Loyalty model, endorsed by Atlantic recording artist Fat Joe, features flat spokes embedded with more than "1,000 Swavorski crystals."

Zab Judah
(Photo Brad Bowling)

Zab Judah spinning
(Photo Brad Bowling)

Devin
(Photo Brad Bowling)

7500 NW 25th St.
Unit A4
Miami, FL 33122
888-OZRACING
www.ozwheels.com

- **compacts**

- **cars**

- **trucks/SUVs**

Since its founding in a small gas station near Vicenza, Italy, in 1971 by partners Silvano Oselladore and Pietro Zen (the "O" and "Z"), O.Z. has designed, engineered and manufactured high-quality alloy wheels for the racing and aftermarket industries. Today, O.Z. sells its wheels world wide for a variety of high-performance vehicles in sizes ranging from 17 to 24 inches. The ultra-thin spokes of its top-line Superleggera series belie the wheel's strength and create a design as beautiful as any in the industry. O.Z.'s Classe wheel features a novel replaceable chrome lip, and there are even models created specifically for SUV application.

F1 Cup
(Photo Tire Rack)

Superleggera 3-Piece
(Photo Tire Rack)

Superleggera
(Photo Tire Rack)

www.pacerwheels.com

- **cars**

- **compacts**

- **trucks/SUVs**

- **street rods**

- **4x4s**

Pacer began making custom wheels in 1972 in Alabama. Since then, it has developed a line of more than 60 styles of steel and alloy wheels. Ranging from 15 to 22 inches in diameter, models include the front-drive Sunburst, Accent, Rush, and Dutch and rear-drive Magnum, Elysium, Shark (which looks like a set of open jaws), and Juice. Steel rims for off-road and 4x4 use include the Rebel, Street Lock, and Black Daytona. The Chrome Rally, Silver Rally, and Chrome Smoothie address the needs of the street rod and older custom crowd.

615C
(Photo Brad Bowling)

Silver Rally
(Photo Brad Bowling)

Sunburst
(Photo Brad Bowling)

Panther/PCW

Prestige Autotech
3366 Pomona Blvd.
Pomona, CA 91768
800-613-8889
www.pantherwheel.com

- **compacts**

- **cars**

- **trucks/SUVs**

P.T. Prima Alloy Steel Universal is another original equipment manufacturer of wheels—Toyota, General Motors, Suzuki, Daihatsu, and several other companies buy from PTP—that expanded into the lucrative aftermarket industry through its Panther Custom Wheels brand. Panther offers 13- to 22-inch alloy wheels finished in a "wet look" silver, mirror polish or high-luster chrome for a variety of American, European, and Japanese vehicles. Designs run the gamut from the dirt-simple five-spoke (EMR 082 and 111 models) to the stylistic craziness of the EMR 204.

PCW
(Photo Brad Bowling)

161
(Photo Brad Bowling)

Platinum

800-232-0734
www.hubcap-tire-wheel.com

- **FWD compacts**

- **FWD cars**

No, they aren't really made of platinum, but this line of 16-to-20-inch alloy rims is awfully shiny. Available in any finish you like as long as it's chrome, Platinum wheels feature imaginatively misspelled names such as Vylator, Vendeta, Krees, and Snyper.

81 (Photo Brad Bowling)

Privat

121 Express Street
Plainview, NY 11803
800-645-3878
www.privatwheels.com

- **luxury sports cars**

König produces the Privat line of "personal alloys" in sizes ranging from 17 to 20 inches in diameter. New for 2003 are the Fahren, Fünf, Schnell, and Zwanzig. Strangely, although Zwanzig means "20" in German, that model is only available in 17- to 19-inch sizes.

Fahren (Photo Privat)

Fünf (Photo Privat)

Schnell (Photo Privat)

Zwanzig (Photo Privat)

strange to most Americans that a wheel company would specialize in that offbeat Japanese car company. Now that the 227-horsepower WRX and even-hotter STi model are enjoying great sales success on these shores, Prodrive is in a great position to sell to the growing number of "Subie" enthusiasts. Its line of 17- and 18-inch alloy wheels are copies of the race-winning designs that have been used by Subaru's rally champions over the years. Built for lightweight performance characteristics, Prodrive's wheels are available in white, silver, anthracite, black, and gold.

Prodrive

The Tire Rack
7101 Vorden Parkway
South Bend, IN 46628
888-541-1777
www.tirerack.com
www.prodrive.com

- **Subaru cars**

- **imports**

Before Subaru brought its rally-winning, all-wheel drive Impreza WRX to the United States, it seemed

Quantum Tek Alloys

12850 Moore St.
Cerritos, CA 90703
877-921-0113
www.qtalloys.com

- **compacts**

- **cars**

This line of all-silver alloy wheels features names like S-05, S-07, and S-14. Wheels range in diameter from 15 to 19 inches.

A European Ford Puma wearing Prodrive alloys. (Photo Prodrive)

RacingHart

Dazz Motorsport
5121 Commerce Dr.
Baldwin Park, CA 91706-1451
626-962-0033
www.racinghart.com

- compacts

- cars

The import crowd is the target market for RacingHart's 17-to-19-inch alloy wheels. Its C4, CP, C2, and MS models are available in silver or chrome—some with polished lips. At the top of this high-tech heap is the Type CR in single- and multi-piece construction. The CR's center package features a semi-enclosed cap assembly with a competition-style dynamic center-lock look.

RH Evolution

Dazz Motorsport
5121 Commerce Dr.
Baldwin Park, CA 91706-1451
626-962-0033, www.dazzmotorsports.com

- compacts

- cars

RH Evolution has a line of 17-to-19-inch alloy wheels aimed primarily at the import and front-drive market. Some of their models—such as the C3, S7, and C2 Evo—catch the eye because their ultra-thin spokes appear too delicate to support the weight of a car. A variety of finishes is offered, depending on model, including silver, white, yellow, chrome, graphite, bronze, and polished.

Rebel

Wheel Country
888-810-6247

- compacts

- cars

Rebel Wheels has models that appeal to the less-showy buyer who wants a good-looking rim in the 14-to-17-inch range. Rebels come in machined/clearcoated and polished finishes.

780 (Photo Brad Bowling)

Roja

www.1010tires.com

- compacts

- cars

Roja produces a line of five- and six-spoke alloy wheels in the 17-to-18-inch diameter range. Finishes for the Formula 5 and Formula 7 series are gunmetal and silver.

Ronal

15692 Computer Ln.
Huntington Beach, CA 92649
714-891-4853
www.ronalusa.com

- compacts

- cars

- trucks/SUVs

Ronal has been making lightweight alloy wheels since 1969; its products have been used as original equipment on virtually every important automobile manufacturer including Mercedes, Audi, Porsche, Saab, Volkswagen, Rolls-Royce, Lotus, Toyota, Nissan, Honda, Mitsubishi,

Ford, and others. Ronal's one- and multi-piece wheels appear on high-performance vehicles from tuning houses Lorinser, Alpina, Carlsson, and Hartge, to name a few. The German company currently offers a line of 13-to-20-inch models for a huge selection of vehicles. Designs include the rounded five-spoke (SL), lace (LS), a triangular center (R24), and a truly whimsical model with a teddy bear for a center (Bear).

Rondell

888.682-3129

www.thewheelexchange.com

- **European cars**

German company Rondell has a line of 17-to-19-inch wheels that fit Mercedes, Audi, BMW, Saab, and Volkswagen cars. The wheels are one- and multi-piece construction and are finished in silver. Each wheel is X-rayed before shipping to check structural integrity.

Rozzi

800-545-5745

www.wheelmax.com

- **trucks/SUVs**

Rozzi wheels occupy the popular "big boy" end of the diameter spectrum, with rims measuring 17 to 23 inches. Like many brands in this segment, you can have any finish you want, as long as you want chrome.

RS Limited

Golden Apple Corporation
3532 Arden Road
Hayward, CA 94545
510-780-9800
www.adrwheels.com

- **compacts**

- **cars**

RS Limited's Ricochet, Nengan, Phase II, Senso, Akunin, Trauma, Ikari, S-Type, Valkyrie, Mase, Concept Pro, and Limix are available in 15- to 18-inch diameters with silver, white, anthracite, gunmetal, chrome, and gold finishes.

Concept Pro
(Photo RS Limited)

Elite
(Photo RS Limited)

Limix
(Photo RS Limited)

Speedline Corse

The Tire Rack
7101 Vorden Parkway
South Bend, IN 46628
888-541-1777
www.tirerack.com
www.speedlinecorse.com

- **compacts**

- **cars**

Speedline Corse produces a line of 16-to-18-inch alloy wheels in a variety of materials and styles. Its product line is made up of four different construction types: one-piece cast magnesium and one-piece, two-piece and three-piece cast and forged aluminum. Most are available in silver or with a stainless trim. The company takes pride in its ISO 9001 and QS 9000 certifications and the 61 world titles and countless national titles obtained in nearly 35 years in all motor racing categories. It is the largest manufacturer of cast magnesium wheels in the world, and claims to be the only company that provides this technology and these high-tech materials for the road.

1908
(Photo Tire Rack)

2113
(Photo Tire Rack)

2110
(Photo Tire Rack)

Mask
(Photo Spintek)

Mask spinner
(Photo Spintek)

Vegas
(Photo Spintek)

Vegas spinner
(Photo Spintek)

Spintek

1455 Columbia Ave.
Riverside, CA 92507
800-864-4387
www.spin-tek.com

- **cars**

- **trucks/SUVs**

"Just because your ride comes to a stop, doesn't necessarily mean your wheels have to." With logic like that, you either love or hate the gimmick of gigantic free-floating spinners that give the appearance of a stopped wheel while the vehicle moves and begin rotating as it slows. If increasing your car's or SUV's unsprung weight by several pounds does not make you cringe, Spintek currently has two high-quality spinner faces that bolt to existing 18-to-24-inch wheels. Assuming you aren't getting enough attention from the current set of $4,000 wheels on your ride, adding a Spintek spinner will definitely boost the "look at that" rate.

Sport Edition

The Tire Rack
7101 Vorden Parkway
South Bend, IN 46628
888-541-1777
www.tirerack.com

- **compacts**

- **cars**

Sport Edition offers a line of 14-to-19-inch wheels with silver, chrome or gray finishes. Its elegant designs, with names like Tekno and Valore, are primarily different takes on the classic five- and six-spoke layout. They are designed and manufactured in Italy.

Fox2
(Photo Tire Rack)

Fox5
(Photo Tire Rack)

Tekno
(Photo Tire Rack)

SporTrux

1439 South Cucamonga Ave.
Ontario, CA 91761
909-923-2664
www.sportruxwheels.com

- **trucks/SUVs**

Only call SporTrux if you want to fill your truck or SUV fender slap full of chromed alloy wheel. The company's "little" wheel is a 20-incher and they only get bigger from there. As much imagination was used in the naming as in the design—Bumpin', Sicker, Trippin', Hater, Pimpin', Baller, Chillin', Binge, Blocker, and Rider make up the SporTrux catalog.

SSR

The Tire Rack
7101 Vorden Parkway
South Bend, IN 46628
888-541-1777
www.tirerack.com
www.speedstar.co.jp

- **compacts**

- **cars**

Although many of the wheels in the SSR catalog are for Japanese Domestic Market and European vehicles, several of its applications are sold in the U.S. as well. Through an exclusive contract with Alumax, SSR is the only manufacturer in the world today producing Semi-Solid Forged alloy wheels—a specialized process whereby uniquely structured alloy billets are heated to a semi solid state (the consistency of soft butter) and molded in a specifically engineered forging press. Its most popular wheels sold in the U.S. run 15 to 19 inches in diameter and come in silver, gold, or polished finishes.

Competition
(Photo Tire Rack)

GT1
(Photo Tire Rack)

GT3 Bright Satin
(Photo Tire Rack)

Tenzo R

Autotech Systems
and Accessories
20758 Centre Point Pkwy.
Santa Clarita, CA 91350
661-251-3409
www.tenzoracingsports.com

- **cars**

- **compacts**

More than a dozen distinct wheel styles are available in the 15-to-19-inch range from Tenzo R. This company creatively and enthusiastically addresses the needs of the tuner crowd, with its high-performance Apex-5, Morphix, Psycho, Sinko, Poke, and AV-7 models offered in a range of finishes—chrome, silver, anthracite, and gold.

Psycho-10
(Photo Tenzo R)

Type-2 (Photo Tenzo R)

Apex-5
(Photo Tenzo R)

Morphix-15
(Photo Tenzo R)

Passion-5
(Photo Tenzo R)

Poke-10
(Photo Tenzo R)

Tezzen

23705 Via Del Rio
Yorba Linda, CA 92887
866-457-6649
www.tezzenwheels.com

- **cars**

- **compacts**

- **trucks/SUVs**

From the same folks that produce Lexani wheels come three 20-to-22-inch chrome monsters—Zenna RWD, Vizzio FWD, and Vizzio RWD.

TSW

Wheel Country
888-810-6247

- **cars**

- **compacts**

- **trucks/SUVs**

The TSW line runs from 15 to 23 inches and includes a wide range of designs, from the simple five-spoke Edge to the busy Ballistic to the "don't cut your finger on that" geometric craziness of the Mayhem.

Ultra

6300 Valley View Ave.
Buena Park, CA 90620
704-994-1444
www.ultrawheel.com

- **compacts**

- **cars**

- **trucks/SUVs**

Ultra alloy wheels range in size from 14 to 22 inches and include a large variety of designs. The Torpedo is a wide six-spoke deep-dish style; the Assault is a notched five-spoke; and the Snyper has the sharp-bladed five-spoke look. Finishes include chrome or polish.

145
(Photo Brad Bowling)

145
(Photo Brad Bowling)

Unique

Wheel Country
888-810-6247

- **cars**

- **compacts**

Unique Wheel makes rims the old-fashioned way—out of steel! Its Smoothie, FWD Mod, D Window, Comet, Rally, Flash, A Window, Sixer, and Supreme all have the hot retro look but without the price of alloys. Most models are available in chrome.

Veloché

The Wheel Connection
530 North Meridian Avenue
Oklahoma City, OK 73107
866-306-0323
866-VELOCHE
www.thewheelconnection.com

- **cars**

- **trucks/SUVs**

Chrome, chrome, chrome is what you get when you buy a set of 17-to-22-inch Ventoso, Jagged, Vio, Spike, Deco, Vandalo, Vela, or Verzio wheels from Veloché.

Velox

749 S. Lemon Ave.
Unit A2
Walnut, CA 91789
888-899-9988
www.veloxperformance.com

- **compacts**

- **cars**

- **trucks/SUVs**

Velox means swiftness in Latin. In physics, it has a meaning the layman isn't likely to understand—just stick with the speed definition. Velox Performance produces the incredibly beautiful Progear (17 and 18 inches), Titan (18 to 24 inches) and VX (17 to 19 inches) series of alloy wheels. Some of its wheels, like the 12.5-pound Progear Pg-5s, are produced under 10,000 tons of pressure for lightweight strength. Most models are available in gunmetal or silver.

Vision Custom Wheels

3512 6th Ave. SE
Decatur, AL 35603
800-633-3936
www.visionwheel.com

- **compacts**

- **cars**

- **trucks/SUVs**

Vision makes polished and chrome wheels in the 15- to 20-inch range for cars and trucks. The company has a line of OEM replica wheels for Mustangs and Corvettes as well as an inventory of discontinued designs.

Volk Racing

9921 Jordan Circle
P.O. Box 4025
Santa Fe Springs, CA 90670
562-946-6820
www.mackinindustries.com

- **compacts**

- **cars**

Volk Racing is the top brand name line of forged wheels from RAYS Engineering, a Japanese manufacturer of high-tech wheels for motorsports and street. They are current wheel suppliers to winning factory race teams of Honda, Nissan, Toyota, and Mazda in tough racing series such as JGTC (Japan Grand Touring Car Championship), JTCC (Japan Touring Car Championship), BTCC (British Touring Car Championship), Formula 3000 and Formula 1. RAYS manufactures wheels for revered factory tuning firms such as TRD (Toyota Racing Development), Mazda Speed, Nismo, and Mugen. Its TE37 wheel is made from 6061 aircraft-grade aluminum, which is hot forged—first with a pressure of 5,000 kilograms per square centimeter, followed by a slow process with 3,500 kilograms per square centimeter. The lip is also forged to 3,500 kilograms per square centimeter. This process allows the wheel to have less material but more strength and durability. TE37 weighs a mere 8 pounds for the 15 x 6.5 wheel and 16 pounds for the 18 x 8.5.

4
(Photo Mackin Industries)

Carino
(Photo Mackin Industries)

CE28N
(Photo Mackin Industries)

ITC
(Photo Mackin Industries)

Sesto
(Photo Mackin Industries)

Spadawide
(Photo Mackin Industries)

Vöxx

Discount Tire Direct
14631 N. Scottsdale Rd.
Scottsdale, AZ 85254
800-589-6789
www.voxxwheel.com

- **compacts**

- **cars**

- **trucks/SUVs**

Vöxx alloy wheels come in sizes 15 through 22 inches and are available in silver, chrome, or polished finishes. The company specializes in the 17-to-20-inch range. Models include Scorze, Brava, Forza, Sparza, Strada, and Argus. They fit most vehicles sold in the North American market but target European upscale BMW, Audi, and Mercedes-Benz customers as well as the Asian-made tuner market of Honda, Nissan, and Toyota.

Scorz (Photo Vöxx)

Turbina (Photo Vöxx)

Matrix 8 (Photo Vöxx)

R Action (Photo Vöxx)

Saga (Photo Vöxx)

Weld Racing

933 Mulberry St.
Kansas City, MO 64101
866-753-4272
www.weldracing.com

- **cars**

- **race cars**

- **trucks/SUVs**

Weld claims to be the world leader in forged alloy wheels. Since it has a wheel for just about everything an enthusiast might do with his vehicle, there is some validity to this boast. Their 4x4 truck wheels—the Crusher, Stonecrusher, Mountaincrusher, Dakar, and Outback, to name a few—are available in every size the serious off-roader could need, and the F-1 series one-piece forged wheel has a no-polish clear finish. Racers covet the Draglite XP, Rodlite XP, Prostar, and legendary Alumastar 2.0 and Magnum Drag 2.0 with Double Bead-Loc protection. Weld's "pretty" wheels are the Evo series targeted toward the less-thrifty Mercedes, Lexus, and Corvette owners. With sizes ranging from 18 to 20 inches, Evo wheels feature names like Andro, Espada, Axis, and Radian.

Typhoon
(Photo Brad Bowling)

Weld 212
(Photo Brad Bowling)

Weld 212
(Photo Brad Bowling

Wheel Vintiques

5468E. Lamona Ave.
Fresno, CA 93727
559-251-6957
www.wheelvintiques.com

- cars
- compacts
- vintage
- trucks/SUVs

Mike Stallings turned a two-car garage and some equipment he bought with a credit card into a multi-million dollar business. Wheel Vintiques produces—and re-produces—a vast array of steel, cast billet, and forged rims for all sorts of vehicles. Sizes run conservatively from 15 to 18 inches, but when you realize how many millions of collectible American cars from the 1950s, '60s and '70s now need a set of reproduction stock wheels, Stallings' business plan becomes a little clearer. Not only does Wheel Vintiques manufacture the most popular factory wheels in

history—including the Rallye, Magnum 500, and every type of "smoothie"—but it makes the hubcaps, rings, and other accessories without which a wheel would be incomplete. Stallings even has a line of retro wheels for Chrysler's new PT Cruiser.

X20

www.x2owheels.com

- cars
- trucks/SUVs

X2O warns you right up front—"Only delivering 20" and bigger!" And does it ever deliver! From the modified five-spoke design of the Spy to the busy geometry of the Blunt and Trauma, X2O wheels are one-piece alloys that only come chromed and range in size from the promised 20 to 23 inches.

Spy (Photo Brad Bowling)

Trauma (Photo Brad Bowling)

Zenetti

800-432-8572
www.zenetti.com

- cars
- compacts
- trucks/SUVs

Zenetti's Tek, Revo, Ice, Mystik, and Saphire come in sizes 17 to 23 inches. Finishes are limited to silver and chrome.

P266 (Photo Brad Bowling)

CHAPTER NINE

AVERAGE JOE BUYS WHEELS AND TIRES

Forget for a moment about the mega-millionaire basketball and rap star vehicles you see on MTV; what you are about to learn is how we normal folks strive for automotive style on a budget.

Not all of us can afford to buy a new $50,000 Cadillac Escalade and drop another $5,000 to $10,000 for a set of triple-chrome 24-inch wheels and 35-profile tires. That doesn't mean, however, we are forever shackled to the rims that looked fine when our car was new but are now so "five minutes ago."

The typical car enthusiast—we'll call him Average Joe—is a guy whose budget for upgrades is nearly non-existent after he's paid for food, mortgage, health insurance, and taxes. Joe is a young adult working full-time to pay his bills, but he's very proud of the bone-stock, five-year-old Mustang V-6 convertible he bought recently and fantasizes about the day his pale pony becomes a stylin' stallion.

(You know Joe, don't you?)

Joe knows that absolutely nothing can change the appearance of a car more profoundly than the proper set of wheels and tires. He cringes a little every time he looks at the skinny 15-inch three-spoke rims Ford installed on his '98 at the factory. As he sits in traffic every day, Joe witnesses a constant parade of Mustangs similar to his wearing a variety of cool rims, and he begins to mentally rank the different designs in order of affordability and desirability.

On the bottom rung of this "ladder of style" is Joe's factory rim; it came on the car and could be considered free. The top rung—Joe drools a little when he thinks about it—is a set of shiny, still-in-the-box alloy rims he saw on a magazine cover car last month.

Joe does some research and discovers that all Mustangs built since the new body style was introduced in 1994 have

Joe's 1998 convertible is super clean, but a little boring. The biggest change he can make to its appearance and performance is the right set of wheels and tires. (Photo Brad Bowling)

the same five-lug bolt pattern—no matter if the car has the base V-6, V-8, or Cobra V-8. During those years, the Mustang wore about a dozen different wheel designs, many of which Joe could live with if the price were right. A few pokes at the calculator tell Joe that his universe of used factory wheels is gigantic, considering Ford produced 1.2 million of its popular ponies with his identical lug pattern since '94. These factory pieces make up the majority of Joe's ladder.

It all seems pretty simple until Joe remembers that most of his wheel choices (anything larger than his 15-inch stock rims) will involve the purchase of tires as well, which means additional expense. Joe's local wheel and tire dealer adds another option to the decision-making process when he points out that any factory rim can be given a whole new look by sending it away to be chrome-plated.

Joe finally commits his ladder to paper before making a decision about what to purchase. Because his budget is a moving target—he can't say for sure how much he can afford until he realizes how much he likes a certain option—he includes some of his less-attractive alternatives as well as the aftermarket wheels he knows he can't afford.

Here is Joe's ladder.

Keep the stock rims - $0
Joe has already determined this option will not do.

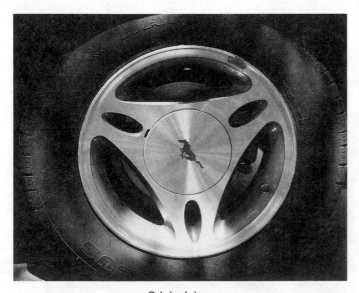

Original rims
(Photo Brad Bowling)

Buy a later set of used Mustang V-6 rims in the 15-inch size - $40-$100
In the case of the Mustang, Ford has spruced up the V-6 wheel since the new body style so there are a few fresh designs to choose from. The reality of the marketplace is that everyone with a Mustang (or any other popular performance car) wants the wider, taller wheels associated with the V-8 models so V-6 owners generally give away or sell cheaply their wheels when they upgrade. This means that Joe could put a different set of same-size wheels on his car by taking his wagon and as little as $60 to a large automotive swap meet.

Buy used V-8 rims and tires - $200-$800
Because of that shared lug pattern among all 1994 and later Mustangs, Joe can literally bolt a new look onto his convertible for as low as $200. Ford knew some of its customers would balk at the idea of paying to replace expensive 17-inch tires on its GTs, so there was also a 16-inch rim offered for several years at the same time. Those 16s are extremely cheap now at swap meets and can often be bought already mounted with good used tires. There

Later 15-inch factory rims for V-6 Mustangs
(Photos Brad Bowling)

Used V-8 Mustang rims (Photos Brad Bowling)

Chromed GT wheel
(Photo Brad Bowling)

have been five or six different 17-inch designs available on the GT since '94, all of which show up on occasion at the flea markets or at Mustang shops as "pull offs" (wheels and tires removed from a vehicle when new).

Have the local wheel dealer chrome the stock V-6 rims - $600-$800

With this option, Joe can be sporting what looks like shiny new custom rims, and he doesn't even have to buy new tires. There may be some down time for the Mustang while his wheels are away at the chrome shop. Scanning the small advertisements in the back of his favorite car magazines gives Joe contact information for companies that offer this same service so he can compare prices.

Buy used Cobra wheels and tires - $800-$1,200

By owning a V-6 Mustang, Joe is avoiding the higher gas bill, insurance, and initial purchase price of a top-of-the-line Cobra. He can, however, enjoy some of that car's high-performance style by shopping around for a set of used Cobra wheels. All generations of Cobra wheels can be found for sale at swap meets, through car clubs, and on that great virtual flea market, eBay. It's even possible to find sets with tires still mounted. Because Ford and SVT produce far fewer Cobras than GTs, Cobra wheels bring a premium, although the earlier models are in less demand.

Buy used GT or Cobra wheels and have them chromed, new tires - $1,500 to $1,800

Joe knows this option is about as close as he can get to a custom wheel without actually shelling out the bucks for it. Again, it will require haunting the flea markets, eBay, and local Mustang club meetings to find the deal that will allow him to stay within his budget. The cost of high-performance tires for 17-inch rims can scare away some folks who have only bought rubber in the past for a Taurus, Lumina, or other grocery-getter. A quick scan of the online tire distributors tells Joe that he'll be spending between $400 to $550 for a set of four Goodyear Eagles, BFGoodrich T/As, Khumo ECSTAs, or Sumitomo HTRs.

Buy new aftermarket wheels and/or tires - $400 to $4,000

This possibility leaves Joe open to do just about anything, but since he likes to dream big, he calculates how deeply he would go into debt by ordering a set of chrome

Used Mustang Cobra wheel
(Photos Brad Bowling)

Sample of chromed factory wheels (Photo Brad Bowling)

BBS RK II wheels and Bridgestone Potenza high-performance tires. The tires measure 245/40-18 on the front and 275/35-18 on the rear and go for about $880 a set. The wheels are 18x8.5 inches on front and 18x10 inches in the rear and will put Joe back $1,700.

Because he hasn't won the lottery yet, Joe realizes he can stay comfortably in the low end of the aftermarket by mounting his current, inexpensive tires on a set of new 15-inch alloy wheels. He locates a 15x6.5-inch rim finished in silver made by Sport Edition. It's a split five-spoke design called the Fox 5 and it costs around $100 a wheel. Having his old tires mounted and balanced on the new wheels will still cost less than a third of the price of his BBS dream package. Joe orders the Fox 5s, gives his Mustang an all-new look, and keeps the factory originals to put back on the car in case he decides to sell it some day.

Before we Average Joes put down good money to upgrade our favorite car's rolling stock—be it our example Mustang or a Honda Civic, Chevy S-10 pickup, Lexus, or some other popular model—laying out all the options on paper is a great way to begin shopping.

BBS RK II 18-inch rims
(Photo Tire Rack)

Sport Edition Fox 5 (Photo
Tire Rack)

CHAPTER TEN
THE VOICE OF EXPERIENCE

Punchy Whitaker

Whitaker Wheel & Tire is history! Well, in the good sense of the word it is.

When bulldozers start rolling and smashing this year on the bustling corner of Concord Parkway North and McGill St. in Concord, N.C., it will mark the end of an era for a company that is as much a vital part of Carolinas car culture as Charlotte Motor Speedway nine miles to the south or the many dozens of NASCAR team shops located within an hour's drive.

Although the scattered collection of ancient, mismatched buildings (a better description might be "sheds" or, less politely, "shacks") is scheduled for demolition, don't look for a new Starbucks-anchored strip-mall to rise up and take its place. Fortunately for longtime Whitaker customers—enthusiasts from every segment of the car hobby as well as regular folks who just come for the good deals on tires for their Tauruses—the company is merely clearing the sacred ground for a shiny modern showroom and warehouse.

Although there's little to commemorate its place in local stock car mythology, none other than the legendary Dale Earnhardt once worked in this building busting tires for Whitaker. (Photo Brad Bowling)

This giant leap into the 21st century is a good thing for Whitaker's clientele, who will no doubt appreciate the new facility's roomy, well-lit display areas, and easy-to-access inventory of the latest wheels and tires. Say goodbye to sagging wood floors punished by decades of heavy stock and the kind of enthusiastic foot traffic retailers dream about. No longer will locating a set of older wheels mean a scavenger hunt from building to building, room to room, trailer to trailer. And what will become of the stacks of "pull-offs"—used wheel and tire sets taken in trade—always parked every morning at the corner of the property like that day's fresh catch right from the boat?

On a busy Saturday, standing as you are within easy earshot of NASCAR's noisy epicenter, it's possible to squint and catch a glimpse of stock car racing's early years—before any driver ever uttered impossibly silly phrases like "my Enron/Qualcomm/Yahoo.com Chevrolet did real good

The company's official name is Whitaker Wheel & Tire, but everybody for 100 miles around just calls it "Punchy's." (Photo Brad Bowling)

in practice" or knew what a "brand loyalty index" was. Busy workers maneuver from shed to shed, rolling tires by hand or transporting them in a variety of ancient conveyances to the tiny garage area where cars are lifted bodily and fitted with new rubber before re-entering the always-in-progress Concord Parkway 500. This is automotive service at its ungarnished best, the way it used to be.

As a point of fact, in a town where it's not possible to shake a tire iron without hitting a NASCAR driver, engine builder, fabricator, or crew member, it should be noted that seven-time Winston Cup champion Dale Earnhardt worked in one of these buildings in the '70s—this brush with a legend has since been commemorated by a framed copy of the Intimidator's last Whitaker pay stub.

Whitaker's is one of those sturdy Southern businesses that has prospered over the years largely by word-of-mouth advertising, like a favorite local diner people will tell out-of-towners about only if they like them.

After talking with "Punchy" Whitaker, the man behind the business, we came away with the impression that it's the people—not the architecture—that made Whitaker Wheel & Tire what it is today. It is clear that Punchy continues to use the oldest business model in the world, one that commonly goes by the name "horse trading." Punchy buys low and sells low, but with a profit built in. Without any sort of high-tech spreadsheet or computer program, he keeps track of wheel trends in various parts of the country—a constantly updated "what's hot, what's not" mental database that allows his company to offer its customers great deals on styles that may be out of favor or not quite caught on yet on the West Coast, for example. The man would be right at home on the floor of the New York Stock Exchange if wheel and tire futures were publicly traded.

We also took the opportunity to get some solid, hands-on advice about buying wheels and tires.

Why "Punchy?"

My father, the man who opened this business in March, 1965, and ran it with my uncle, was called "Punch." Somehow, my older brother and I acquired the nickname as well, which made things confusing at times if all three of us were in the room together.

I got out of high school in 1972 and went to college for two years. When I came back my daddy added on to one of the warehouses and opened up what we called Whitaker Wholesale. We started buying a little bit in quantity and saving money that way. We had about a 2,500-square-foot building in a shopping center across the street, so we moved the whole wheel department over there. Business has been strong ever since.

In the early days of this business what qualified as "speed equipment?"

You had your old Keystone, Cragar, American Racing

The "main" building, which currently houses the office, showroom, and service desk, will remain after the other structures are leveled for Punchy's new construction. (Photo Brad Bowling)

wheels—they were some of the first. Cragar licenses other companies to produce certain wheels for it now—Keystone is part of Cragar. American Racing is also still around. Those brands are a lot more expensive now than they were then, but they are pretty economical compared to others.

Since you didn't have an Internet to look stuff up back then, it was difficult sometimes to know how well certain equipment would work on different vehicles. I remember when I was about 12 years old my sister's boyfriend had a '65 Plymouth Fury III. We were putting a set of Keystone wheels on it. We had two on one side and were getting ready to go to the other side—none of us knew Chrysler products had left-hand lugs [through 1971]. We had to order more lugs before we could take the Fury off the jack stands.

Today, we still run into problems that are unique to a certain application, especially around these large brakes cars have today. It's pretty rare, though, considering how many aftermarket wheels we sell.

Back then, was the aftermarket wheel business a substantial part of the company?

You could buy a whole lot more with a dollar back then, and most tire stores were strictly in the tire business. I can remember back in the early '70s during the gas shortage when people weren't driving as much and the tire business slowed down, but folks kept buying those wheels.

And that was at the end of the era when people had to buy tires once or twice a year because they didn't last too long. The wheel business normally stays strong even in bad economic times. For most people, a wheel upgrade is something they want—not something they need, and people don't mind spending money on something they want.

That still holds true today. If somebody works hard making that money, their car comes first, especially if they are single.

In the late '60s, how much did a decent set of aftermarket wheels and tires cost?

You were probably looking in the $300 to $350 range. It's odd, but tires really aren't much more expensive now than they were then, and they last 10 times longer. You can still buy a cheap set of good radials today for $150, but a set of bias-ply tires would run over $100 in the '60s. Of course, recaps would sell for $15 a pop.

Tires are some of the few products that are a better deal than they used to be.

How did your business change, and how did the overall industry change?

A lot of different styles came out in the '70s. Anything in chrome was still pretty popular—always has been—the old American wheels with the gray centers sold well. The industry didn't change so much in the '70s a whole lot, but when you get into the '80s, with the return of performance and introduction of front-drive vehicles, it changes.

Wheels for Toyotas, Datsuns, Volkswagens, and those other popular imports had to be re-designed for offset and other factors. BBS made a sharp-looking mesh wheel that was really popular.

Did you ever think people would be putting 24-inch wheels and 35-profile tires on their vehicles?

No, I didn't really think it would catch on at first because it looked kind of funny. Now, when you have a regular Escalade or Tahoe wearing 16s [stock 16-inch wheels], it looks strange. I didn't really see that coming.

I can remember back in the late '80s when Superior came out with a "soft-spoke" wheel to fit front-drive cars. The rep came in with them and said, "These are going to be big sellers." A set of them retailed for $600. At the time, I didn't think anybody would pay that much for those wheels, but we stocked them anyway. After a while, we couldn't get enough of them.

Of course, "hammers" and "stars" were big sellers in the late '80s, early '90s. Cragar made a five-spoke star for front-drivers that went for about $350 a set—then the soft-spoke came out, basically the same as the five-spoke polished wheel. Chromed, they ran about $700 to $800 a set. We sold those things like crazy, then the style faded and slowed down.

In the mid-'90s, everything started changing as companies looked for new styles. Today, it's gotten kind of crazy with all of the new designs and gimmicks.

Speaking of trends, it's interesting to notice that the Cragar S/S sells better today than it did when it was new.

Do you advertise your company? How much of your business is based on word-of-mouth?

In the last year or so, I've been in the process of building a new facility, trying to get through the loopholes with the local government. We're going to build a 15,000-square-foot showroom for the inventory. The building will have 35,000 square feet on seven or eight acres with a warehouse in back. We're tearing down these old buildings here, except for the one on the corner.

I'd say for the last 10 years we have done a little bit of advertising in the newspaper. We've always had a large out-of-town business because of our large inventory. About 90% of our sales come from customer referrals.

In the last year we've done a little TV advertising, using a co-op fund through companies we buy from. We might as well use it.

We've built a good reputation over the years for having a good inventory and selling at a good price. The key is in how you buy your stock. We watch for a lot of deals. A lot of times manufacturers will over-produce or in certain areas of the country certain styles won't be selling so strongly—that's when it's a good time to buy at a discount. Usually if 100 or 200 wheels are available, we can move them.

Most of your chain dealers advertise a lot, but they don't have as much product in the store. Nobody can have everything in stock, but if it's fairly popular and sells well, we try to have it on hand. It costs a lot these days to keep an inventory up.

What cars and trucks do you keep in inventory? Obviously, you don't have a lot of Peugeot or Yugo wheels on hand...

Right, the most popular vehicles for the really large stuff—the 20s to 24s—are General Motors SUVs, like Escalades and Tahoes. The six-lug bolt pattern on those is still our best seller. Now, your Expeditions and Lincolns, up until this year, were a 5 x 135 [number of lugs and millimeters in diameter measuring the circle of lug holes in wheel] and it's been a little soft lately, although it's always been as much as 30 to 50% of what we were selling in GM stuff.

Ford decided this year to go to a six-lug pattern, but used something different than 6 x 5.5 [inches], which has been out since the '40s. They went with a 6 x 135—totally new. Ford and Lincoln are pretty bad about changing stuff for no reason, like when they changed the eight-lug truck pattern in '97. Instead of 8 x 6.5, they went to 8 x 170, which was about the difference of one thread on the lug.

As far as keeping the inventory current with all the different sizes, it's a constant chore to keep stuff up to date. A lot of your Maximas and Cadillacs have 17-inch wheels; your Corvette has 18-inch wheels. Dodge has had a 20-

inch wheel for a while now. We were having trouble getting BFGoodrich's 24-inch tire because—rumor says—Dodge is supposed to be building a truck with a 24-inch package on it and BFG was supplying them first. I haven't seen it, though. They've built some wild and exotic stuff, so I wouldn't doubt it.

Keeping in stock a wheel with a 4 x 100 bolt pattern—a lot of small cars still use that—and 5 x 4.5, like on Maximas and Lexuses is a safe bet. GM makes a 5 x 115, which is a hair off of 5 x 4.5. A lot of people can run one or the other. As far as stocking wheels, most of them that have caps covering the lug nuts run two different bolt spreads on the same wheel. Sometimes you can take one set of wheels and have them fit as many as 10 different cars.

We used to say we had over 10,000 wheels in stock. Now that they are so much more expensive, that number has dropped some, but the quality and variety have gone up. I've got over 100 sets of 20-inch wheels—different styles of wheels—that average cost anywhere from $225 to $250 apiece. That market got competitive among makers, then it got soft. 24s are still extremely high, though.

What's the hottest wheel design out there right now?

"Spin" wheels are really hot right now. They are made in two parts—the wheel itself, and then a giant spinner that floats on a ball bearing hub attached to the center. When you are driving down the road the spinner, which is about

What once was a good billboard advertising the company has long since faded from exposure to the elements. Fortunately, word-of-mouth keeps enthusiasts aware of the company's location. (Photo Brad Bowling)

the size and design of the wheel behind it, stands still. When you apply the brakes, the centrifugal force causes the outside plate to start rotating, which makes it look like you are going 30 miles an hour while sitting at a stoplight.

A company called Davin originated this idea. A set of those Davin spinners retail for close to $11,000 or $12,000—that's without the tires. Omega builds a copy, and there are some bolt-on kits you can buy, but still you are going to spend $4,000 to $5,000 even on something cheap.

I like to show off my inventory on my personal cars sometimes so I had a set of 22-inch Isis wheels and spinners (installed) on my Escalade. I bought a clear trailer that I put a wheel display in so we can get some interest in our products at the mall or at shows. I pulled the trailer in our recent Christmas parade behind my Cadillac and it got a lot of attention. That Sunday, at church, my preacher even brought up that his grandson wanted his paw-paw to buy a set for his truck.

How much fun would it be to change a flat on the side of the road with one of those?

With some of those spin-type wheels, it takes a few minutes to get the Allen head screws out, but it's not too bad.

Are there a lot of real-world problems associated with extremely low profiles on tires?

We try to tell a lot of parents who are buying for their kids that it's not really practical to have a tire with an inch and a half or two inches of sidewall because if you hit a pothole you can damage the wheel. People get a little ill sometimes because they think the manufacturer is supposed to make that good when they get damaged. We try to help in those cases when we can. A lot of major companies will work a courtesy deal and at least sell them for half price. There are places out there that will repair the wheels, but there is a little bit of a liability involved.

With the roads in the conditions they are in, it's surprising we don't get more damaged wheels in here. You know, sometimes the damage is hidden, though. We get cars in here where the wheel and tire look great, but when we pull the tire, you can tell somebody went off-roading by

mistake.

The smaller the sidewall and the bigger the wheel, the less cushion you have to play with. I guess people pay pretty close attention to their driving when they spend $5,000 for a set of wheels.

What's the most expensive thing you've done on a customer car?

I'd say the spin wheels—the Davins. With a set of 24-inch tires, the bill runs close to $15,000.

It's not something you sell every day. What used to seem like an outrageous sell a few years ago—the $2,000 to $2,500 sale—is daily now. I've sold as many as 10 sets of 20-inchers on a good Saturday. The average wheel and tire dealer doesn't keep that kind of stuff in stock like we do, so that helps us make the sale when you can drive in, pick out your new wheels, and drive them home.

Who are these customers who spend $2,500 on impulse for new wheels and tires?

Mostly it's the kids still in school. A lot of them work to make some money, and sometimes the parents help out with their purchase. It's gotten a lot more common in the last year for kids to buy their own. It used to be mostly people like ball players and people who made a lot of money—business people.

In the last 30 days, I sold a set of Omega spin wheels to a gentleman in his 50s for his 14-year-old boy. The parents are driving the car now, until their son gets old enough to get his license.

Another couple in their 60s had an older style Cadillac Escalade, and I had a set of regular 22s they really liked. The Cadillac place told them they would have problems putting anything more than a 20 under their car. I think that's just because the Cadillac place didn't have anything larger in stock. Anyway, that couple came down here and said they wanted something that would really make their Escalade stand out from the crowd, so they drove home on their new wheels and tires.

A good wheel dealer sells everything—from the 24s down to these custom chromed golf cart rims. (Photo Brad Bowling)

Do these gigantic wheels not affect the suspension and ride, especially on heavy SUVs?

They are gigantic. Realize that a 23-inch wheel is bigger than what an 18-wheeler runs—they run 22.5s, most of them.

You would think it would be worse than it is, but if they are balanced correctly and the tires don't have any flaws, it's just like any other set. It's been my experience—and I've owned a lot of cars and wheels—that ride doesn't suffer any more than if you put on a set of heavy-duty shocks.

We were concerned at first with these spin wheels because they weigh so much. So far, though, everybody has been tickled with them. I would have thought that something you bolt on after you balance the tires—the big spinner goes on after—would really affect the ride, but it doesn't seem to.

I've got 23s on my car now. The tire's just as smooth as when it was new, so it doesn't show any signs of imbalance— you just have to be more careful when you install them to get everything just right.

What is the stupidest thing anyone has ever asked you to do to their car?

We've probably got a lot of stories on that, but I guess the funniest thing I remember is the fellow who had a set of five-lug wheels he had bought from another person and wanted us to install them. His car had a six-lug pattern, though. When I pointed that out, he asked if we could just knock one of the studs off to make the wheel fit.

We still laugh about that story.

In the old days, people used to run aluminum wheel adapters, which I try to steer people away from. They use them sometimes to install knock-off wheels—the kind that you have to tighten up with a hammer—on a car that wasn't meant for them. We try to stay away from that kind of setup, because we don't want somebody coming back a few months after working with us and saying their wheel came off.

For a while there, customers would come in wanting to put wheels made for rear-drive cars on their front-drive cars, which makes the wheel stick way out from the body. People were putting 13x7-inch reverse wires on and looking like they were driving a roller skate going down the road. That fad didn't really last too long around here, although it seemed to hang on out west.

The tires wore out quickly because there was no good way to align the wheels with that kind of setup, and the suspension really suffered.

The same alignment problems occur today because people have lowered their cars so much that the suspension and steering components just can't accommodate it.

I don't really know how much more radical it can get.

As for customers making unusual requests, I would have to say that we occasionally get someone in with, say, a rusted-out Caprice from the '70s and they want to spend $4,000 on wheels and tires when the car itself is only worth about $200 or $500.

Punchy has owned many collectible and custom cars—almost always wearing the latest custom rims. Ironically, this Mercury street rod sits on steel wheels and Cadillac hubcaps. (Photo Brad Bowling)

If someone has a really outrageous request that we don't think will work very well, we don't put it on. We don't want customers to have problems.

Everybody is different as to what sacrifices they will accept to get the look they want. You might have one guy who wants a bigger tire that rubs just a little when he makes a sharp turn; he says it's no problem. The next guy with the same car might find that unacceptable. The first guy has it in his head that he wants that particular look for his car, and he'll work with it, even if it means taking a hammer to the fender when he gets home.

You mentioned knock-offs, the kind of single-spline wheel that used to be seen a lot on '50s Jaguars and '60s Cobras and Corvettes. Do you really get many customer requests for those?

You'll see a lot of 120-spoke wire wheels on older Caprices, Cadillacs, and other big luxury-type cars. There's a cone that bolts on to the factory lugs. That cone is the converter hub for the knock-off. That system can be a lot of trouble.

Knock-offs may look cool on certain cars, but there is a very good reason every auto manufacturer switched to a lug-mount system. Lugs are much more secure.

A few years ago, one of our local car collector dealers used to run a lot of '60s Corvettes through here to get new tires put on factory knock-offs. One time, we drove the car around in the lot after putting the wheels on and we tightened them a second time after that—just like you are supposed to. That car didn't get three miles back to the dealership before one of the wheels worked itself loose.

These days, about 99% of the cars we get in here have an acorn-type lug nut, which is a really good design that reduces the chance of a nut backing itself off. There are some classic styles we sell like the Cragar SS and Keystone that take a mag lug, which rides flat against the wheel instead of going down into it. Either way, they are safer and easier to maintain than knock-offs.

The best piece of advice I give to customers is that they should re-torque their wheels 15 miles after they leave our shop, and again at 100 miles.

What is a problem you see a lot from customers that would save them money if they would change something they are doing?

A big problem we see, and this is something that's not really the customer's fault so much, is that people take their cars with chrome wheels through a car wash and the machine automatically sprays an acidic solution on the hot wheel, which streaks the chrome. On a polished aluminum wheel, you can clean it out, but there's not a lot you can do about chrome in that case.

That's one of the most common things we see. We've had car washes replace wheels for people. It can affect a plain stock wheel with a clearcoat.

A lot of people will scrape a curb with a wheel and ask they can get it replaced for free because the chrome "went bad." It's funny when you can see concrete particles still in the gouge.

We noticed in your showroom an 18-inch Corvette wheel and tire, which looks huge sitting on the car, but it's next to a 24-inch SUV combo and looks tiny. You can't really tell how a setup will work until it's sitting under the fender, can you?

A lot of kids lower their cars and trucks because they want a tire to fill up the fenderwell. Take the Chevy S-10 pickup. The only way to take out the empty air in the back is to bring the body closer to the ground and put a bigger tire; otherwise, it just doesn't look right no matter what you do with the tires.

When Dodge first came out with its new Ram in 1994, the rear fenderwell sat 10 inches above the tire—2 or 3 inches of space is fine. It never looked quite right with the stock setup. Everybody wanted a bigger tire to try to fill it in, like a 285/75-16 on the stock wheels.

Do you sell mostly high-performance equipment out of here or is it bread-and-butter stuff?

Mostly high-performance. If you drive around any new car lot anymore, you'll see that most vehicles worth driving already have alloy wheels and low-profile tires. It seems like the whole industry has copied the aftermarket.

Your average person comes in with a factory 205/60-15 on his Maxima, and that's what he wants a direct replacement for in tires. That's not really a high-performance application these days, but 10 years ago, that was a sporty tire.

Do you get a lot of street rod business?

Yeah, it's changed a lot over the years, but it still requires more specialized attention to pick out wheels and tires for a street rod because each one is different. Wire wheels were popular 20 years ago with that crowd. Cragar made a true wire wheel that was pretty successful—most were simulated wires.

In the '90s, most street rodders went to a billet wheel. Most want to run 14 or 15 [inches] in front, with a 15-incher in the rear—later, they moved to 18- or 20–inch wheels in the rear.

When you are talking about a car that somebody has modified to his own specifications—the suspension is not set up like anything you've seen before; the fenders are all different sizes and clearances—a guy can talk all day on a Saturday in here trying to find what he likes and what's going to fit. There have been all kind of devices invented to help with fitment issues like this, but they really don't work as well as mounting a tire on a wheel and bolting it on the car.

Those wires you've mentioned... Do they require any kind of spoke tightening or special maintenance?

Not any more. A lot of your really old stuff needed that kind of adjustment—especially bicycles and motorcycles. The worst part of those old wire wheels is that they leaked air like crazy. It was common to see silicone sealer packed around where the spoke entered the rim. Of course, people also used a wide band made of rubber to keep air from going out the spokes, but those would wear out and get holes in them eventually.

A lot of wires are actually tube-type wheels. I've got a '56 T-bird with a 15-inch McLean wire wheel on it. It's a front-lace wheel, all front-laces had to have tubes in them. (Absolutely no off-set and the wheel is narrow so it will fit under the vehicle—front-lace.)

What is a "chrome reverse" wheel?

It's really just a name for a deep-dish stamped steel wheel that's been chromed. Originally, It was applied to factory wheels that were turned around so that the offset was changed and the tire would stand out a little wider from the body.

Do you ever get requests for specialty items like magnesium wheels or reproduction pieces for classic cars?

Most specialty items are something a customer can order from a national company as cheaply as we could get it from them. For example, Coker Tires makes some of the best reproduction classic tires, but they aren't set up to work through independent retailers. Their customers can order through a catalog or buy online, just like we would have to. We prefer people do that, so the warranty is directly associated with that company.

We deal more with large companies that need distributors for their products, but we'll install anything that our equipment can accommodate.

Do you deal with two-piece or three-piece high-tech wheels?

Sure. We sell a lot of Löwenharts; we keep a set or two of those in stock. I've got a set out here now for a late-model Corvette. They go for $6,500 with Pirelli tires on them. The new Corvette has 20-inch rear, 19-inch front. The set I've got has 200 miles on it, which means I can sell it used for below my cost. The guy who bought them decided he wanted another car, so we bought them back at a lower price because, technically, they were used.

That's one thing we do for people that a lot of shops probably wouldn't do. Sometimes you like something when you buy it, but want something different a few months later. You will lose money—just like with anything it's worth

less used than new.

We try to make the customer happy with his decision right up front, though, so we don't get too many "buybacks." We'll do the courtesy of bolting a wheel on a guy's car if he's really interested, but doesn't know for sure if he'll like it on his car.

Are there a lot of other stores that deal in trades on these wheels?

No, it's kind of unusual. Your chain stores wouldn't want to handle used product because you have to be hands-on to really know what you've got and what it's worth. Nobody watches your money like you watch it.

If you have a used set of wheels, all your money and profit on the deal is tied up in there until someone cleans them up and sells them.

You can probably count on one hand the dealers on the East Coast who do it the way we do it, usually in your bigger cities.

Now, there is a downside to keeping the inventory of new and used wheels that we do. For example, I scrapped 5,000 wheels last year—not damaged wheels or bad wheels, just wheels that were obsolete or not part of a complete set. Sooner or later, you run out of room.

Right now, I've got someone who comes by and picks up our aluminum wheels and takes them to a place in Statesville, where they are recycled. All we have to do is pull the balance weights and stems off.

With factory wheels, you might have a set of 1990 Camaro wheels sitting around that nobody wants because everybody who likes that particular look already has a set. I hate to do it, but eventually it's better to scrap them so they can be recycled than to let them pile up.

I see a lot of chrome factory wheels in your showroom. Are those big sellers?

Most of your wheels that come from the factory are silver. GM and a few others offer some chrome options, but it's rare. At one time, I had 150 different styles of wheels that we had sent out for chrome-plating. Right now, we've got about 75 styles, just because it's not as popular an option.

One reason to chrome a stock wheel is because after about three years of driving them, the clear starts to fail and they look a little milky. That just looks bad on a nice, clean car. For anywhere from $650 to $700, you can make them look shiny and new again. We'll do exchanges if it's something we've got in stock; otherwise, we'll send yours out.

We used to send a lot to California, now we send most of our stuff to Grand Junction, Colo.

We've got about every late-model Mustang wheel in inventory chromed. You are pretty safe with Camaro stuff and wheels from popular trucks, like the S-10 and Tahoes. With trucks, however, that has slowed some because most people looking to upgrade want the really big equipment.

A lot of dealers like having access to chromed factory wheels. We do a lot with Corvettes and keep them in stock all the time. For the last six months to a year, everybody with a Corvette has wanted the Z06 wheel. Because of that demand, it makes the stock Corvette wheel not worth very much.

With recent Mustangs, you can get factory wheels ranging from 15 inches to 18 inches.

What is the difference between chrome and polished aluminum—in terms of reliability and quality of shine?

The real difference is the upkeep. With chrome, you just splash a little soap and water and it looks good. An aluminum wheel picks up a certain amount of dirt, which can stain the aluminum. A guy can polish a set and they'll look good, but they won't stay that way. Chrome is more money, but in the long run it's a lot easier to take care of. Polished wheels can be repolished if you get "curb kisses."

What about some of the new run-flat technologies? Do you deal much with them?

Not that much, considering how much the tire companies advertise it. You know, Uniroyal has a NailGard, General had a Gen-Seal, Goodyear has Run-Flats. A lot of your Corvette owners can currently buy a non-Run-Flat for half of what a Run-Flat goes for.

The price has come down some on that technology,

though. Some people don't mind paying extra for the security of a flat-free tire.

Do people still pick a tire brand and stick with it?

A lot of people have been sold on Michelin over the years and still ask for it by name. A lot of folks like Goodyear. We do a lot of tires for NASCAR racers and teams, and Goodyear is really popular with them because they sponsor a lot of racing.

Some guys from Dale Earnhardt Inc. brought a new Tahoe down here Saturday with Firestones on it; they wanted Goodyears, so we traded with them. I guess it's not really the case that if a Goodyear rep sees another brand on your car that you will lose their business, but I think it doesn't hurt to use their product if you are in that position.

Michelin is our most-requested tire probably. When radials first got popular in the '70s, Michelin had been making them for a while. They were ahead of the game then. Their light truck tires are hard to beat. You pay a little more for them, but they are worth it.

A lot of people come in, though, and are looking for the best deal they can get on a set of tires to get their car back on the road safely. They don't necessarily care about the brand name. Today, with so much computer development going into tire production, it's hard to get a bad tire from a brand name manufacturer.

Do you just keep all of this information in your head?

Some of it stays up there, but there are so many changes to keep track of that it's impossible for any one person to know it all. I keep a lot of catalogs around because they have a lot of useful information about what was offered when. They come in handy when I've got three identical wheels, but no fourth can be found. I threw away 20 sets of three this year.

Thanks for sharing your thoughts with us. Good luck on the new building.

Thanks for coming by.

A

ABS – also known as anti-lock brake system; prevents lockup of any single or combination of wheels on braking and increases steering control under low-traction conditions

accelerator – a chemical used to reduce curing time and speed the vulcanization of rubber

activator – a chemical used to initiate the vulcanization process when making the rubber compound

adjustment – predetermined amount of money allowed the customer on replacement of a tire under warranty

air pressure – force exerted by the volume of air in a tire; in English standards, expressed in pounds per square inch (psi) or kilopascals (kPa)

alignment – checking and adjusting of a vehicle's caster, camber and toe settings to maintain optimum performance

alloy – in the wheel world, alloy is synonymous with aluminum, although for a time magnesium was used to create lightweight wheels

The use of lightweight alloys has resulted in some beautiful designs, such as this ALT Trax rim. (Photo ALT)

alpha-numeric sizing – introduced in late 1960s to categorize broader range of sizes and aspect ratios; ex. F60-15, whereby the letter indicates recommended load capacity, the aspect ratio is 60% - all fitting on a wheel measuring 15 inches in diameter

all-season tires – indicated by M+S, M/S or M&S marking on the sidewall; may also show a mountain/snowflake symbol indicating severe snow capabilities; all-season tires are designed to be used year round

This F60-15 Goodyear Polyglas GT is an early example of alpha-numeric sizing. (Photo Brad Bowling)

anti-roll bar – a steel bar that links the left and right suspension components under a car in order to transfer weight to the outside tire during cornering

antioxidant – a chemical used in production of the tire's tread and sidewall that prevents surface oxidation (rust)

aquaplane – condition that exists when the tread of a tire cannot make direct contact with the road due to a layer of water

aspect ratio – also known as the series; percentage of sidewall height divided by tread width

ASR – known in English as anti-slip control; computers limit power to certain wheels under acceleration on low-traction conditions

asymmetric tires – feature a tread pattern that, when viewed straight on, is not the same on the left half as the right

autocross – motorsports competition over a small- to mid-size course marked by pylons; also known as a gymkhana

auxiliary supported run flat systems – a unique wheel-and-tire combination

The aspect ratio indicates how tall the sidewall is in relation to the tire's width. (Photo Goodyear)

The Falken Azenis Sport has an asymmetric tread pattern (Photo Falken)

that employs a support ring attached to the rim in case of pressure loss; will not work with conventional tires

axial play – the motion of a ball joint moving up and down

This Z06 Corvette is a good autocross car because it has a low center of gravity and exceptional handling. (Photo Goodyear)

Axle (Photo Brad Bowling)

axle – the real or imaginary line between a pair of wheels on the front or rear of a car or truck

B

back spacing – measurement, usually in millimeters, from the wheel's mounting pad to the inner edge of the wheel

balance – using small weights to achieve uniform distribution of mass in a wheel and tire combination in order to reduce vibration

bale rubber – the form in which manufacturers receive rubber before processing

ball joint – ball-and-socket connection that allows a steering knuckle to move in several directions

ball lug seat – type of lug nut or bolt that recesses into the wheel lug opening for a snug fit; shape is semi-circular

banbury – machine that grinds and mixes various components to create rubber compound used in the production of tires

basketweave – a wheel design that uses and intricate pattern of straight, interconnecting lines; also known as lace

bead lock – a device used to clamp a tire bead against the wheel rim with mechanical force, as opposed to air pressure alone; used by serious off-roaders

This cutaway of an ALT Echo alloy rim shows an example of back spacing. (Photo ALT)

Balancing (Photo Brad Bowling)

Basketweave (Photo Goodyear)

Bead (Photo Coker)

to keep wheel and tire together at extremely low air pressure under low-traction conditions

bead – the hoop of high-strength steel that squeezes the tire against the rim

bead seat – point at which the tire rests against the inside of the wheel rim

belt edge wedge – rubber placed beneath the edges of a belt on a tire; improves durability on radial tires

belted bias – tire with additional reinforcing belt or belts between casing plies and tread

belts – bands of cords that run beneath the tread surface

bias ply – a tire carcass reinforced by embedded fabric cords that criss-crossed each other from bead to bead across the underside of the sidewall and tread

bladder – rubber bag filled with steam under pressure; used during tire production to press the tire into the mold from the inside out

blem – short for "blemish;" a tire with a non-structural deformity; usually sold at discount

body – tire structure other than rubber in tread and sidewall

bolt circle – diameter of an imaginary line connecting the center of each lug opening in a wheel

Bolt circle (Photo Brad Bowling)

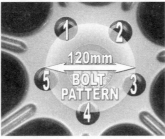

Bolt pattern – 5 x 120 (Photo Brad Bowling)

bolt pattern – the number of lug holes in a wheel <u>and</u> the diameter of the bolt circle in inches or millimeters; ex. 4 x 5.12 or 4 x 130

braking torque – force applied by brake to stop movement of wheel and tire under load of vehicle

breakaway – point at which there is no longer traction while cornering

buffing – removing a portion of a tire's tread through grinding, similar to shaving

bump steer – when toe or camber changes such as during a bump that affects the steering

---

C

---

calendar – one of the first machines in the tire-making process, a calendar produces a thin ply of rubber compound from two or more rolls

camber – degree to which the tire tilts away from vertical; zero camber describes tires standing perpendicular from the ground; negative camber means the bottoms of the tires are farther apart than the tops; positive camber has the tops of the tires farther apart

carbon black – a reinforcing filler agent that increases wear resistance when mixed in the tread compound

carrying capacity – based on inflation pressure, the amount of load a tire can carry

casing – also known as the carcass; the plies and bands that give structure to the tire

caster – the difference between a line perpendicular from the ground and the imaginary line drawn through the upper and lower ball joints; positive caster increases low-speed steering input but helps high-speed stability

Center bore (Photo Brad Bowling)

center bore – the large hole in the middle of the bolt circle; in hub-centric wheels, it is machined to exactly match the car's hub; with lug-centric wheels, it is usually a generic size to fit a number of vehicles

center of gravity – imaginary point on a vehicle where weight is perfectly balanced front to rear and side to side

centerline – imaginary plane that divides a wheel or vehicle into symmetrical halves

centrifugal force – force pushing an object away from the center of rotation

chafer – rubber-coated material with high abrasion resistance applied to tire's bead to prevent chafing against bead seat or rim flange

chains – the last resort for most people in low-traction winter situations; a system of cables or chains draped over the car's drive wheels

Chapman strut – basically a MacPherson strut for the rear of the car

coefficient of friction – indicates the difficulty of sliding one surface against another

cold inflation pressure – the volume in a tire that has driven less than 1 mile or has not been driven for three hours

compounding – in tire manufacturing, refers to the combination of rubber, carbon black, plasticizers, curing materials and ozone retardants to form the visible part of the product

concave molding – occurs when the tread is depressed during manufacturing; when inflated it lies flatter against the road

Crown (Photo Goodyear)

conical lug seat – type of lug nut or bolt that recesses into the wheel lug opening for a snug fit; shape is wider at head and tapers to a smaller diameter in the direction of the wheel

contact patch – also known as the "footprint;" the area of tire rubber supporting the weight of the vehicle and making contact with the road; low-profile tires tend to have wide but short patches, whereas high-profile models contact the road with long, narrow footprints

control arm – connects the unsprung components to the sprung chassis; allows suspension travel

cord – the basic component of a ply or belt

cornering force – lateral pressure applied to a tire by a cornering vehicle

cross pattern – system for tightening lug nuts that spreads out the torque pressure

cross section width – distance from one sidewall to the other, not counting any raised areas or lettering

crown – circumferential center of a tire's tread

crowned road – when pavement is elevated in the middle to allow quick drainage of water

curb guard – a rubber lip or ledge that runs around the tire just above the whitewall to prevent scraping the white area

curb kiss – scratch or gouge resulting from a wheel's contact with a concrete curb or other immoveable object

curb weight – weight of a vehicle with full fluids and no passengers

---

D

deflection – difference between a tire's loaded and unloaded shape

design rim – what manufacturers mount tires on to measure dimensions

DOG TRACK (uneven axle)

Dog tracking (Photo Brad Bowling)

Diameter (Photo Brad Bowling)

diameter – vertical measurement of the wheel from one point on the bead seat to its opposite

directional stability – tendency of a tire to roll in the direction in which it is steered

dog tracking – also known as crabbing; when the rear wheels do not follow the path of the front wheels

DOT – short for Department of Transportation; seen on tire sidewalls to indicate compliance with that department's guidelines

double A-arm – suspension system with upper and lower A-shaped links from the wheel to the chassis

dual compound tread – when a tread is designed with two different rubber compounds

duals – two wheels joined on one side of an axle

dually – a truck with dual wheels in the rear

durometer – gauge to measure the hardness of rubber

dynamic balance – balancing the tire while it is spinning on a machine

---

E

ECE – short for Economic Commission for Europe; indicates compliance with

Five-spoke wheel (Photo Tire Rack)

Interco Super Swamper flotation tire (Photo Interco)

standards relating to physical dimensions, tire branding and speeds

ESP – also known as Electronic Stability Program; combines all the characteristics of anti-lock braking, anti-slip control and yaw control to detect and correct critical driving situations such as oversteer or skidding

ETRTO – European Tire and Rim Technical Organization

extrusion – forcing a mass through a fixed opening to create a length of material

---

F

fiberglass – material used in construction of tire belts; a mixture of fine spun glass and adhesive

five-spoke – one of the most common wheel designs, so-called for its five simple or ornate spokes radiating out from the center

flat lug seat – type of lug nut or bolt that presses directly against the lip of the wheel's lug opening

flotation – a wide tire, usually for trucks and tractors, that "floats" by minimizing penetration of dirt

footprint – also known as a contact patch; that part of the tire's tread that actually contacts the road surface under load

forging – forcing billet aluminum between forging dies under pressure; results in great density, strength and lightness

---

G

GROOVES

Grooves (Photo Continental)

g – a symbol that represents the acceleration of gravity

gravity casting – most common and cheapest method for creating alloy wheels; uses gravity to fill the wheel mold with molten aluminum; not desirable if lightweight properties are necessary for application

green tire – a complete tire that has not been cured by heat and pressure

groove – a channel that runs between ribs of tread to expedite transfer of water away from the tire's contact area

gross axle weight rating – also GAWR, the maximum weight designated for the front or rear axle

gross combination weight rating – also GCWR, total weight of tow vehicle and loaded trailer

gross vehicle weight – also GVW, the total weight of the loaded vehicle

gross vehicle weight rating – also GVWR, maximum allowed loaded weight of the car or truck; must not exceed GVWR

H

high-pressure die cast – manufacturing technique for wheels; places tremendous pressure on aluminum alloy to create shape

hub centric – a design wherein the center bore of the wheel is machined to a specific size; allows the hub to support the weight of the vehicle and center the wheel

hub centric ring – a nylon insert used during installation of non-hub centric wheels to keep the wheel properly placed

hydroplane – also known as aquaplane; occurs when water cannot be displaced from the tire's footprint in time for the tread to make solid contact with the road

hysteresis – when energy is applied to a tire through cornering or rolling resistance, heat is generated

---

I

imbalance – when distribution of mass in a tire is uneven and results in vibration

independent suspension – when the car's four suspension packages are attached to the chassis but not to each other

inertia – tendency of an object to remain at rest until acted upon by an outside force

innerliner – the part of a tire most responsible for retaining air under pressure; made up of soft layers of rubber

JDM cars (Photo Volk)

J

JDM – shorthand for Japanese Domestic Market; very popular segment of the Japanese import tuner crowd; can refer to whole cars not available in the U.S. market or certain parts of those cars, such as engines, suspension components and wheels

---

K

kilopascals – symbol is kPa; metric unit of air pressure – 6.89 kilopascals equal 1 pound per square inch

---

L

lateral runout – side-to-side motion of a rotating wheel

lead – when the vehicle pulls to one side while attempting to keep a straight line

leaf springs – stacked series of thin steel plates bolted together to allow suspension under compression

Lower sidewall (Photo General)

---

lift points – all modern vehicles have these designated platforms for the attachment of hydraulic lift plates so as not to damage the chassis underneath

load – the weight pressing against tires any time the vehicle is resting against the ground or at speed

load range – a system for classifying the load capacity of truck tires that replaces the old ply count system

load rating – when applied to a wheel, refers to the maximum weight it is designed to support

lower sidewall – the part just above the tire's bead

low-pressure casting – positive pressure moves molten aluminum into the wheel mold; most common process for OEM wheels

lug centric – until recently, the most common form of wheel design; the weight of the car rests against the lug nuts themselves, instead of the vehicle's hub

Dunlop SP Winter Sport M2 M+S (Photo Tire Rack)

Mount pad (Photo Brad Bowling)

MOUNT PAD

M

M+S – also M/S and M&S; indicates a tire meets the Rubber Manufacturers Association qualifications for use in mud and snow

MacPherson strut – a single unit composed of a shock absorber, upper steering pivot and wheel spindle

mag – short for magnesium; a misnomer still applied to wheels that are made of aluminum alloys

match mounting – procedure for aligning the high point (heaviest spot) of a tire with the low point of a wheel in order to balance them out

mount pad – flat area on the inside of the wheel that presses against the vehicle's drum or rotor surface when mounted

---

N

NailGard – Uniroyal's brand name for its puncture-resistant technology; the company claims such tires can re-seal after 90% of common punctures up to 3/16-inch in diameter

Negative offset (Photo Volk)

negative camber – when the tops of the tires on a same axle are closer than the bottoms, as viewed from the front

negative caster – occurs when the upper pivot point of the suspension is behind the wheel's steering axis

negative offset – simply put, when more of the wheel's rim sits outside the mounting pad, away from the vehicle; technically, when the mounting pad is behind the centerline of the wheel; commonly referred to as a "deep dish" design; common in older rear-drive cars, pickups and SUVs

NHTSA – National Highway Traffic and Safety Administration

---

nominal – indicates that one tire's dimension is considered the same as another tire's dimension because the differences would have no noticeable effect on performance

numeric sizing – early, very limited system for measuring tire dimensions; prevalent during post-WWII period through 1970; ex. 6.95-14, whereby the tread width is 6.95 inches, wheel diameter is 14 inches and sidewall aspect ratio is assumed to be industry standard 90%

O

OEM – shorthand for original equipment manufacturer; many aftermarket wheel producers also supply the world's automobile factories; OEM status carries a certain implication of quality standards

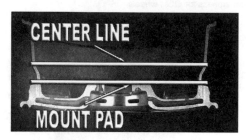

Offset (Photo ALT)

offset – distance in millimeters or inches from the mounting pad of the wheel to its centerline; zero offset occurs when the mounting pad sits exactly on the wheel's centerline

One-piece wheel (Photo Kosei)

one-piece – most common type of aluminum wheel, whereby face and rim are cast together

Overall diameter (Photo Continental)

overall diameter – the diameter of a properly inflated tire bearing no weight load; as measured from crown to crown

overinflation – air pressure above recommended level; can increase handling response, but also gives a more jarring ride to the vehicle and can expose the tire to damage

oversteer – when the rear tires lose traction in a turn at speed before the front

oxidation – rust, essentially; can apply to rubber compounds that begin breaking down due to exposure to oxygen and the elements

---

P

---

pitch – distance from a point on one tread block to the same point on its closest neighbor; pitch can be adjusted during the design process to minimize noise

ply – reinforcing layers of cord fabric and rubber in a tire

plus sizing – allows bigger diameter tires to be mounted with lower-profile tires so as to keep the rolling circumference and original ride height the same as stock; "plus 1" refers to a wheel diameter increase of one inch, "plus 2" is a two-inch increase, etc.

P-metric sizing – modern standard for measuring tire dimensions; ex. P185/75-

14, whereby the tire's tread width is 185 millimeters, the sidewall aspect ratio is 75% and the wheel diameter is 14 inches

pneumatic – a system that uses a rubber bladder or casing filled with pressurized air to reduce shock in a tire; John Boyd Dunlop is credited with its invention, although records indicate a Scottish engineer had developed the idea earlier

polyester – synthetic cord material in casing construction; chosen for its light weight and strength

positive camber – the bottoms of two tires on the same axle are closer than the tops, as seen from the front

positive caster – occurs when the upper pivot point of the suspension is ahead

Positive offset (Photo Borbet)

of the wheel's steering axis

positive offset – simply put, when more of the wheel's rim sits inside the mounting pad, toward the vehicle; technically, when the mounting pad is outboard of the wheel's centerline; common in front-drive vehicles
PSI – pounds per square inch

pyramid belt – belt design where the bottom layer is wider than the upper layer

pyrometer – measures tread temperatures

R

---

rack-and-pinion system – a steering system composed of a gear at the base of the steering column and a rack of steel teeth

radial play – when a ball joint can move from side to side

radial tire – so-called because the ply cords "radiate" straight up from the tire bead to cross to the opposite bead; this system is further enforced by a belt of steel fabric running the circumference of the tire

rayon – used in casing and belt construction; a synthetic cord that chosen for its high dynamic strength and good adhesion to rubber

recirculating ball – where steering is transferred through a gearbox; seen a lot on older cars

repacking bearings – a service whereby grease is squeezed in the wheel bearings

retread – a used casing to which a new tread is attached

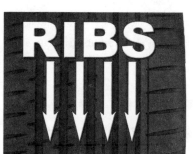

Ribs (Photo General)

revolutions per mile – number of revolutions a tire makes in the course of one mile

Ride height (Photo Volk)

Rim drop (Photo Billet Specialties)

rib – part of the tread that contacts the ground, oriented in generally straight lines around the circumference of the tire

ride height – distance between vehicle frame and road

rim width – measured from bead seat to bead seat

rim diameter – overall diameter of the wheel's bead seat

rim drop – lowest point of the wheel's inner surface area

rim flange – outermost edge of the rim; also known as the lip; usual mounting place for balancing weights; the victim of most "curb kisses"

RMA – Rubber Manufacturers Association

road wheel – a piece of laboratory test equipment used to simulate the road surface

rolling resistance – the capacity of a tire to gain and maintain momentum; lower resistance results in higher gas mileage

rollover – when a tire's sidewall bends enough under cornering forces to contact the pavement

Rotate Wear Indicator (RWI) – Kumho Tires' system available on certain models that provides visual cues to the owner that it is time to rotate the tires; these pinhole-sized indicators also detect uneven tread wear

rotation – the practice of moving tires from one corner of the vehicle to another in an established pattern so as to reduce tire wear

rubber-to-void ratio – difference between the rubber are and the "empty" groove area in a tire's footprint

rubbing – what happens when a tire makes contact with a fender or exhaust pipe while in motion

run-flat technologies – any number of systems produced by tire and wheel manufacturers to prevent loss of stability or mobility in the event of total loss of pressure; generally accomplished through the use of a stiffer sidewall; some require the use of onboard tire pressure monitors

runout – how far out of round a tire is that it cannot be balanced

---

S

---

safety bead – raised area located adjacent to and inboard of bead seat

SEALIX – Firestone's self-sealing, puncture-resistant technology

section – either an imagined or literal slice of a tire from one bead, across the tread, to the opposite bead

section height – distance from the bead to the crown of a mounted and inflated tire without load

section width – widest part of the mounted and inflated tire, as measured from the sidewall

self-aligning torque – it's why a wheel returns to a straight-ahead position after being turned while in motion

semi-solid forging (SSF) – accomplished by heating a billet of aluminum to nearly liquid, then forcing the material into a mold at a high rate; cheaper than forging, but similar in results

series – also knows as profile or aspect ratio; refers to the second piece of numeric information in a P-metric tire size; in the example P225/60R15, the section height of the tire is 60% of the section width, making the example tire a 60 series

service descriptions – a description required on speed-rated tires, excluding Z-rated models, that follows the P-metric size; ex. P245/45-R15 87S, whereby 87 represents the load index (in this case 1,201 pounds) and S refers to the speed rating (in our example, 112 mph); service descriptions have been mandatory since 1991

shaving – reducing a tire's tread with a blade while spinning; usually performed for competition
shimmy – rapid wobble of a tire in motion

Shoulder (Photo Mastercraft)

Sidewall (Photo General)

shoulder – territory between the tread and sidewall of a tire

shoulder gauge – the measurement of rubber thickness in a tire; more than any other part of the casing, the shoulder affects the running temperature of the tire

sidewall – flexible portion of the tire between the bead and the tread

sipe – tiny slits molded into the ribs of the tire tread to improve wet traction

silica – a reinforcing filler used with the rubber compound to reduce wear and rolling resistance

skid resistance – ability to maintain traction on any surface while in motion

slip angle – difference between direction a tire is steered and direction of tire travel

slot – a groove in the tire's rib and shoulder areas designed to aid wet traction

speed rating – indication of a tire's high-speed durability when measured on equipment under a controlled, indoor environment

sprung weight – every part of the car that is supported by the suspension

spun-rim casting – also known as "rim-rolling" technology – a multi-stage process whereby a wheel begins with low-pressure mold injection, gets spun at high speed, has its outer portion heated and then is pressed by steel rollers against the rim area to achieve final shape; result is similar in strength and weight to forging, but not as expensive

squirm – when a tire's footprint deforms momentarily due to thick tread and

Star pattern (Photo Brad Bowling)

excessive loading

stability – the tendency of a car to maintain a curve without swaying

stacked belt – where two or more belts are the same width, one atop the other

star pattern – recommended procedure for torquing lugs on a five-lug wheel
static – not moving

static balance – condition in which a wheel/tire assembly shows no unequal weight distribution while still; opposite of dynamic balance

steel belt – the component most responsible for the stiffness of a tire casing, comprises the outer circumference of the tire, just below the tread

steering response – how long it takes for the car's direction to change once the driver has turned the steering wheel

sulfur – key component of the rubber vulcanization process

suspension – components working together to support the weight of a vehicle on its axles

synthetic rubber – technology originally developed to replace rubber if needed during wartime; used today in many applications, including the production of tires

Temporary spare (Photo Brad Bowling)

Tread (Photo Continental)　　**Tread void (Photo Goodyear)**

tracking – how straight the vehicle goes down the road; based on its relationship between the rear wheels and imaginary center line of the vehicle

tread – that part of a tire designed to rest against the ground

tread pattern – how blocks and grooves are arranged to form the tread

tread void – channels and grooves designed into the tire to force water away from the road contact point

treadwear – useful life of a tire tread

truck jerky – slang for large strips of shredded tractor trailer tread lying on the road after a tire failure; so-called for its resemblance to beef jerky

tubeless – a tire whose inner liner removes the need for a separate inner tube

Tuner (Photo Volk)

T

temporary spare – sometimes known as a space-saver spare; designed for limited use under emergency situations; not intended to be driven on full-time

tensile strength – how much pulling force can be applied to a material (such as the cord or belt in a tire) before it fails

three-piece – wheel face is created separately from the two parts that make up the rim; after construction, all three components are joined, usually with a sealant to prevent loss of air

tie rods – arms that join the steering system to the steering arms that change the direction of the vehicle's wheels

Tire & Rim Association – also known as T&RA or TRA; one of the bodies that develops guidelines for tire and wheel makers

tire mixing – combining tires from different manufacturers or of different sizes, compounds or purposes; not recommended on the same axle; some vehicle manufacturers do not recommend it at all

toe – distance between the front and rear of opposing tires; if closer together in the front, "toe-in" results; "toe-out" happens when rears are closer

toe-out turn – when the inside wheel of a car is angled more sharply than the outside wheel during a turn

torque – in the wheel world, tightening lug nuts to a force specified by the manufacturer; should be done manually with a torque wrench on alloy wheels to prevent warping from over-tightening

torque rating – specified pressure measured in foot-pounds

torsion bar – a stiff arm designed to twist under load like a spring

TPC – Tire Performance Criteria; a mark indicating approval of certain General Motors specifications for OE use

track – distance between tires on the same axle

tuner – a compact car modified with lightweight, high-performance components; introduced to middle America by the popular movie The Fast and the Furious

Tread wear indicators (Photo Falken)

TWI – or tread wear indicators; also known as wear bars; equally spaced raised ridges located at the base of the tire's main grooves designed to become visible when the tread has worn to 2/32-inch

two-piece – most popular of the new multi-piece wheels; face and rim are created separately, then joined

U

underinflation – when tire pressure does not meet the manufacturer's specifications; can lead to overheating of cords and failure

understeer – when the front tires lose traction in a turn at speed before the rear

undulation – wavy appearance on the sidewall of some properly inflated radial tires; considered normal effect of cord and ply bonding

uni-directional tires – due to tread design, designed to be used effectively only in one direction; arrows on the sidewall indicate intended direction of installation

unsprung weight – weight of all components not supported by the suspension; wheels, tires and brake components are classified as unsprung weight

Uniform Tire Quality Grade (UTQG) – a labeling system required by the Department of Transportation that standardizes treadwear, traction and temperature resistance ratings on tires; not required on winter or light truck tires

V

valve – device used to let air in or out of a tire

variable integrated pitch – a tread design feature created to reduce road noise by changing angles and pitch of tread block elements

vulcanization – the process of heating rubber with sulfur; developed in 1839 by Charles Goodyear

W

waddle – technical term for movement of a damaged wheel or out-of-round tire that causes the footprint to shift left to right while the vehicle moves straight ahead

wander – when a car veers or drifts away from a straight line against driver input

wear bars – also known as treadwear indicators or TWI; located at the base of the main tread grooves, equally spaced around the tire; designed to be easily seen when tread has worn past its useful life

Wheelbase (Photo Borbet)

wheelbase – measurement taken from the center of the front wheel to the center of the rear wheel

wheel bearing – a component that fits between the wheel and spindle to allow free spinning movement; most common is tapered roller type

wheel weights – a variety of small, carefully measured ingots attached to the inside or flange of the wheel by clip or self-adhesive backing

Z

zero offset – occurs when the distance from the mounting pad to the centerline of the wheel is exactly zero

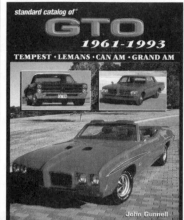
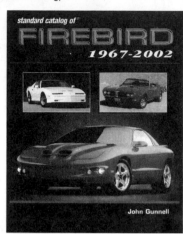
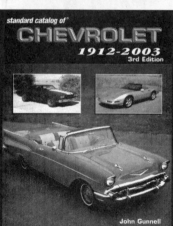
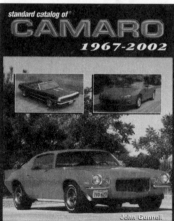